A Gift For

_____

From

_____

Backlist, LLC, a unit of
Chicken Soup for the Soul Publishing, LLC
Cos Cob, CT
www.chickensoup.com

Chicken Soup for the Soul

Woman to Woman

Women
sharing their
stories of
hope, humor,
and
inspiration

Written and compiled by

Jack Canfield and
Mark Victor Hansen

edited by Amy Newmark

This edition published in 2012 by Hallmark Gift Books, a division of Hallmark
Cards, Inc., Kansas City, MO 64141 under license from Chicken Soup for the Soul
Publishing, LLC.
Visit us on the Web at Hallmark.com.

CSS, Chicken Soup for the Soul, and its Logo and Marks are trademarks of
Chicken Soup for the Soul Publishing LLC.

The publisher gratefully acknowledges the many publishers and individuals who
granted Chicken Soup for the Soul permission to reprint the cited material.

ISBN: 978-1-59530-611-1
BOK1261

Chicken Soup for the Soul

Woman to Woman

Women
sharing their
stories of
hope, humor,
and
inspiration

Written and compiled by

Jack Canfield and
Mark Victor Hansen

edited by Amy Newmark

Chicken Soup for the Soul

Contents

❶
~Women Making a Difference~

❷
~True Friends~

❸
~Special Moments~

❽
~Achieving Your Dream~

❾
~ Taking Time for Yourself ~

❿
~ Gratitude ~

Woman to Woman

Women Making a Difference

Act as if what you do makes a difference. It does.
~William James

The Touch of Kindness

I've seen and met angels wearing the disguise of
ordinary people living ordinary lives.
~Tracy Chapman

"Why do you want to be a nurse, Patricia?"

The two nursing instructors and the dean of nursing sat at their table, squarely facing me as I sat on my hard, straight-backed wooden chair facing them. "Two thousand young people have applied to our program." The dean's voice came from across the room, "and we will select sixty of them. Tell us why we should choose you." She folded her hands and looked up at me from the stack of application forms.

I hesitated a moment, wondering what the other applicants sitting in this same chair had answered. What did they say that was music to the instructors' ears? I tried hard to imagine what they wanted to hear from me.

I thought my reason for wanting to be a nurse sounded simple and silly, so I hesitated and was quiet. It seemed laughable that I should be applying to nursing school at all. During my childhood, I was terrified of doctors, nurses and hospitals. I dreaded every office visit even for an annual checkup! So it was a surprise to many that I now had the desire to become that which I had formerly done my best to avoid. But an incident from my childhood was compelling me, and I drew upon that now.

When I was six years old, my parents were told I needed to be admitted to the hospital for some "tests." They drove me to the children's hospital across town on a cold gray Sunday afternoon. I looked up at the imposing building and then quickly hid my face in my mother's sleeve. I tried to resist going in, but my mother and father were holding my hands and I was whisked along against my will.

We exited the elevator, and my parents led me down a long hallway. When we came to a large room that was divided into cubicles, we stopped. We were directed to one of the cubicles by a stern grayhaired nurse who pointed here and there, showing us where my suitcase should go, where my pajamas and robe should hang, where the button was to press so a nurse would come when we wanted.

My father went downstairs then, and my mother tried to make me feel at home. The gray-haired nurse soon brought a supper tray, but I couldn't eat. Everything here was so different from what I was used to. So my mother picked at the food on my tray while she tried to entertain me. She tried to cheer me by talking about how some of the children there were very sick, and it was nice that I was only there for "tests" and would be able to come home soon.

I wondered why my mother didn't have a suitcase with her. Wouldn't she need some pajamas and a robe, too? After the nurse took the tray away, I learned why. My parents were not allowed to stay with me. They were going home, and I was staying there. They were leaving me, and I'd never been away from them before. As my mother slipped into her coat and prepared to leave, I began to cry.

"No, no, Mama, please don't go, please don't leave me!" I begged. She just smiled slightly and told me she'd be back tomorrow, to be a good girl and do what the nurses told me.

As I listened to her footsteps fade away, I turned over in my bed and curled up in a tight little ball, facing away from the door. I tried to think of something happy. I tried to think of songs I liked to sing. I tried to remember the faces of all my stuffed animals at home. I thought hard, but my thoughts were interrupted by another nurse who said firmly, "Time for bed."

I sat up then, and she removed my robe and pajamas and dressed me in a hospital gown. I lay back down and curled up tighter than ever and wept. The lights were turned out then, and I lay awake in the dark.

Much later, I heard someone enter the room, where I still whimpered in my bed. "You're not asleep yet?" a pleasant, quiet voice asked.

"I can't sleep," I said, trembling.

"Sit up a minute and talk to me," the voice coaxed. I sat up then, and in the dim light I could see it was a nurse, but not one I had seen before.

"I want to go home," I said, sobbing again. The nurse reached forward and held me as I cried. "I think I'm going to be sick," I moaned, and my stomach began to heave.

She held a basin in front of me and wiped my face gently with a damp washcloth. She cradled me then as I calmed down, and I lay limp against her shoulder as she rocked me back and forth.

After what seemed like a very long time, she looked down at me and said, "I have some work to do now, so I can't stay with you." Seeing my dejected look, she added, "But maybe you could come and be with me. Let's see."

In the hallway there were low wooden wagons with mattresses and pillows that the nurses used to take some of the children outside for some fresh air. She brought one of these to my bedside and beckoned for me to get in. As she lifted me down to the wagon, I looked at her shiny name pin and read "Miss White."

Miss White wheeled me out to the nurses' station and parked the wagon by the desk. I watched as she sat and wrote, and every once in a while she'd look over at me and smile. "Want something to drink now?" she asked. I nodded and sipped the apple juice she brought, and soon I drifted off to sleep. Early in the morning she rolled me back to my bed, and I was so tired that I hardly noticed when she told me goodbye.

My mother did come to see me later that day, and the next night was not quite as hard to bear. I had to stay in the hospital for only a few days before my brief ordeal was over. But I never forgot how terrified I felt, and I never forgot Miss White's kindness to a desperately lonely and scared little girl.

This incident ran quickly through my mind, and I thought for a moment before I answered the dean's question. Why did I want to be a nurse? I straightened up in my chair and lifted my chin and said, "Being a patient in a hospital is a frightening thing, for anyone. Some people conceal it better than others, but all patients are afraid. I remember being a frightened child in a hospital when I was only six, and there was a nurse there who was very kind to me. She was the one who made my stay bearable."

The room was quiet as I went on. "I have always remembered her, and I want to be the kind of nurse she was. I want to be the one who cheers up a frightened child, holds the hand of a lonely older person, soothes the anxiety of a nervous patient."

I was accepted to the nursing program and worked hard to learn the skills and techniques necessary to provide the best care for my patients. On graduation night as I stepped up to the stage to accept my diploma, I thought of Miss White and smiled. She would never know what a profound influence she'd had on me. She taught me the most important lessons in nursing. She taught me the significance of empathy for the patient and his or her plight, of compassion in easing the difficulty of another. What she gave to me was now my own to give, the gentle touch of kindness that makes the difference to our patients and to our world.

~Tricia Caliguire
Chicken Soup for the Nurse's Soul

Now I Lay Me Down to Sleep

A mother's arms are made of tenderness and children sleep soundly in them.
~Victor Hugo

Growing up, I wanted to be a doctor, but money was scarce, so I went to nursing school. In 1966, during my senior year, an Army Nurse Corps recruiter came to talk to us. It all sounded so exciting: I would have a chance to travel, it paid well and, most important, I was assured that I wouldn't have to go to Vietnam if I didn't want to—which I didn't.

I signed up. After basic training, I was assigned to Letterman Hospital at the Presidio of San Francisco. During my two years at Letterman, I received orders for Vietnam three times. The first two times, I said no. But the third time, I decided that my two years of experience would probably be a huge asset over there.

We landed in Tan Son Nhut Air Base, and when the airplane door opened, I nearly fell backward, overwhelmed by the heat and the stench. Suddenly, all my experience seemed trivial. Being twenty-three years old seemed very young. I was scared, but there was no turning back.

After our debriefing, I was assigned to the Sixty-seventh Evac Hospital in Qui Nhon. When the helicopter landed on the hospital tarmac, my things were set on the ground. I climbed out, straightening my skirt. The soldiers in the helicopter yelled, "Good luck, Captain" as they took off.

I was in my class A uniform, which meant I was also wearing nylons and high heels. Nothing could have been less appropriate for the surroundings. Miles of barbed wire, topped by concertina wire, encompassed the hospital compound and the large adjoining airfield, along with acres of hot concrete. I squared my shoulders and marched inside the grim cinder block building in front of me. I was told to get some sleep, because I started tomorrow. I gratefully fell into a bed, and in the morning, I donned my hospital uniform—fatigues and Army boots—just like the soldiers.

Because I was a captain, I was made head nurse on the orthopedic ward, which primarily held soldiers with traumatic amputations. I took my role very seriously and had a reputation for strictness.

Being a nurse in the States for two years did not adequately prepare me for Vietnam. I witnessed a tremendous amount of suffering and watched a lot of men die. One of my rules was that nurses were not allowed to cry. The wounded and dying men in our care needed our strength, I told them. We couldn't indulge in the luxury of our own feelings.

On the other hand, I was always straight with the soldiers. I would never say, "Oh, you're going to be just fine," if they were on their way out. I didn't lie.

But I remember one kid who I didn't want to tell. The badly wounded soldier couldn't have been more than eighteen years old. I could see immediately that there was nothing we could do to save him. He never screamed or complained, even though he must have been in a lot of pain.

When he asked me, "Am I going to die?" I said, "Do you feel like you are?"

He said, "Yeah, I do."

"Do you pray?" I asked him.

"I know 'Now I lay me down to sleep.'"

"Good," I said, "that'll work."

When he asked me if I would hold his hand, something in me

snapped. This kid deserved more than just having his hand held. "I'll do better than that," I told him.

I knew I would catch flak from the other nurses and Corpsmen, as well as possible jeers from the patients, but I didn't care. Without a single look around me, I climbed onto the bed with him. I put my arms around him, stroking his face and his hair as he snuggled close to me. I kissed him on the cheek, and together we recited, "Now I lay me down to sleep. I pray the Lord my soul to keep. If I should die before I wake, I pray the Lord my soul to take."

Then he looked at me and said just one more sentence, "I love you, Momma, I love you," before he died in my arms—quietly and peacefully—as if he really were just going to sleep.

After a minute, I slipped off his bed and looked around. I'm sure my face was set in a fierce scowl, daring anyone to give me a hard time. But I needn't have bothered. All the nurses and Corpsmen were breaking my rule and crying silently, tears filling their eyes or rolling down their cheeks.

I thought of the dead soldier's mother. She would receive a telegram informing her that her son had died of "war injuries." But that was all it would say. I thought she might always wonder how it had happened. Had he died out in the field? Had he been with anyone? Did he suffer? If I were his mother, I would need to know.

So later I sat down and wrote her a letter. I thought she'd want to hear that in her son's final moments, he had been thinking of her. But mostly I wanted her to know that her boy hadn't died alone.

~Diana Dwan Poole
Chicken Soup for the Veteran's Soul

One Life at a Time

Some see a hopeless end, while others see an endless hope.
~Author Unknown

As our car slowly made its way through the crowded streets of Dhaka, Bangladesh's capital of 2 million people, I thought I knew what to expect. As leader of the American Voluntary Medical Team (AVMT), I had seen great suffering and devastation in Iraq, Nicaragua and Calcutta. But I wasn't prepared for what I saw in Bangladesh.

I traveled there with a group of AVMT doctors, nurses and other volunteers after a series of devastating cyclones hit the tiny country in 1991. More than 100,000 people had been killed, and now, because flooding had wiped out clean water and sanitation systems, thousands more were dying from diarrhea and dehydration. Children were dying from polio and tetanus, diseases nearly forgotten in the United States.

As we drove to the hospital where we were to set up a clinic, I thought I knew what we were up against: humid, scorching days, heavy rains and crowded conditions. After all, since Bangladesh became independent from Pakistan more than twenty years earlier, some 125 million people lived in an area slightly smaller than the state of Wisconsin.

I glanced out the window at the street teeming with people: men talking in groups, women dressed in bright red and yellow saris, and children chasing each other, darting in between the many carts and rickshaws.

Then I looked more closely. The people were walking through raw sewage. A man stepped over a body in a doorway, just as one of the many body carts pulled up to haul it away. At a busy corner, I saw a woman standing very still, holding a small bundle, a baby. As I watched her face, she pulled her shawl back slightly, and I clearly saw her baby was dead. I suddenly thought of my own healthy children at home, and tears stung my eyes. I'd never seen anything so horrible.

The following day, I decided to ride out to Mother Teresa's orphanage in old Dhaka. A friend had asked me before I left home to visit and see what medical help they needed.

Two of the Little Sisters of the Poor greeted me at the gate and immediately led me to the infant floor. I was astonished to find 160 babies, mostly girls, squalling for attention from the few hardworking sisters.

"There are so many," I said, amazed.

"Some were given up because their parents couldn't feed them," one sister said.

"And others were abandoned because they are girls," said another. She explained that often females are killed at birth because they are considered inferior in the male-dominated culture. What little food there is must go to males.

The irony struck me hard. These baby girls were society's throwaways, yet what had I seen today? Women everywhere: working in the rice fields outside the city, herding children through crowded Dhaka, trying to earn a living by selling trinkets on the street, and here, at the orphanage, caring for the forgotten.

"A couple of the babies have serious medical problems," the sister said. "Would you like to see them?"

I followed her down a row of basket-style cribs to the tiny, sick little girls, both about two months old. One had a heart condition, the other, a severe cleft lip and palate.

"We can't do much more for them," the sister said. "Please help them. Whatever you can do will be a blessing."

I held each baby, stroking each girl's soft, dark hair and gazing into their small faces. How my heart ached for these innocent angels. What kind of a future did they face, if they had a future at all?

"I'll see what we can do," I said.

When I returned to the clinic, hundreds were waiting for treatment and much work needed to be done. I'm not a medical person, so my job was varied: I ran the pharmacy, tracked down medicine when we ran out, negotiated with local officials for equipment or transportation, and scouted the patient line for critical cases.

By day's end, my head was swimming. The helpless babies' cries and the hundreds of faces on the streets and in our clinic all seemed to express the same thing—hopelessness. The thought startled me. These people were without hope. Even Calcutta had not seemed so bleak. Without hope. I repeated the words in my mind, and my heart sank. So much of what AVMT tries to do is give hope.

My inspiration was a woman who had dedicated her life to giving hope to others—my grandmother. We called her Lulu Belle, and she practically ran the Mississippi River town of Cairo, Illinois. She wasn't the mayor or a town official, but if a jobless man came to her back door, she'd call everyone she knew until she found the man work. Once, I came through her kitchen door and was startled to find a table full of strangers eating supper.

"A new family in town, Cindy," she said, as she set the mashed potatoes on the table and headed to the stove for the gravy. "Just tryin' to give 'em a good start." I later learned the man hadn't yet found work, and Lulu Belle was making sure his family had at least one hot meal every day.

Lulu Belle had great faith, and it made her stronger than any woman I knew. Her favorite Bible verse was a simple one: "Do unto others as you would have them do unto you." She believed that if you treated people right, the way you would want to be treated, God would do the rest. So she never worried about where the job or the food would come from—she knew God would provide it.

But God seemed so far away in Bangladesh. I struggled with that thought at our morning meeting. We were set up in a clinic near

Rangpur, in the northern part of the country, and our team had gathered to go over the day's schedule. At the meeting's end I told them what I tell every team: "Remember, we're here to give hope." But the words caught a little in my throat as I wondered how we would do it. Where would hope come from for these people, especially the women, so overwhelmed by disease, poverty and circumstance?

Already, 8,000 people were lined up for treatment. Scouting the line, I noticed something peculiar. All of them were men, many quite healthy. Not until I reached the end of the line did I see any women and children, and most of them looked very sick, some near death. My heart pounded as I realized what was happening. The men expected to be seen first, even if they were perfectly healthy. The women could wait.

I wondered what I should do. I remembered the woman I'd seen on the street, holding her dead baby, perhaps because she couldn't get care quickly enough. I thought of the abandoned babies in the orphanage, and anger and frustration welled up inside me.

Maybe a bit of Lulu Belle was with me as I rushed past the line and back inside the clinic to tell the doctor in charge what was going on. He was as upset as I was.

"Well, what do you think?" he asked. "We can either see all these well men, or we can get the sick women and children up front."

"Let's do it," I said. "Let's do what we came here for."

I ran back outside and asked the interpreter to tell the men at the front to step aside. He did, and immediately I heard a disgruntled murmuring rumble through the crowd. The men were angry and the women were afraid to come forward. The interpreter repeated the announcement, and as we tried to get the crowd to move, a scuffle broke out and soon soldiers appeared, their guns strapped across their chests. They tried to restore order, but several men still pushed to the front of the line.

"Tell them no," I said to the interpreter, gathering all the courage I had. "Tell them we treat the sick women and children first or we fold up the clinic."

The men looked at me for a moment, then backed down and

began letting the women forward. The fear and sadness I'd seen on the women's faces gave way to joy as they rushed to enter the clinic first. They smiled at me, grasping my hands and arms in thanks.

As one woman stretched out her hand to give me a flower, our eyes met, and I saw something incredible: hope. Now I understood. We didn't have to pull off a miracle. It was what my grandmother believed about doing unto others what was right. And out of that simple act, God had brought life-affirming hope.

Our doctors and nurses saved lives that day, and treated thousands during our two weeks in Bangladesh. When it was time to come home, I returned by way of the orphanage, to bring the two sick babies I'd seen back to the United States for treatment. On the plane home, I knew I'd have a surprise for my husband—that we would be adopting one of them, now our beautiful Bridget.

Several months later, I had the privilege of meeting with Mother Teresa about Calcutta's medical needs. In her beautifully simple way, she crystallized what I had felt in Bangladesh.

"How do you deal with the overwhelming needs, the disease, the death?" I asked.

"You look into one face," she said, her voice filled with peace, "and you continue the work." And know that God will do the rest.

~Cindy Hensley McCain as told to Gina Bridgeman
A Second Chicken Soup for the Woman's Soul

Voice in the Night

How wonderful it is that nobody need wait a single moment before starting to improve the world.
~Anne Frank

When I was nineteen years old, my friend Hanneke Boogaard was studying to become a nurse at Beatrix Hospital in The Netherlands. There, nursing students work during their study, the same as regular personnel. During her work on the night shift, Hanneke was strangely drawn to one patient in particular, a forty-year-old woman in a coma. Because Mrs. Groensma never had visitors, Hanneke remained at her bedside longer than the others. At first she tried not to admit it, since for her all patients should mean the same. But this woman fascinated her.

When Hanneke heard the patient had no living relatives, she spent even more time with her. She'd learned that people in comas could sometimes hear when they were spoken to. This woman had no one to do that for her, so Hanneke talked softly to her every night. Since she didn't know her, she didn't know what to talk about, so she told Mrs. Groensma all about herself. She explained how her parents had died in a car crash when she was young. For hours she shared her many memories of them. That's all she had to cling to now. How she wished she had a specific personal item to remember them by—the golden four-leaf-clover locket her mother always wore. It was lost during the accident and never found, even though relatives searched the crash site and nearby ditch. Night after night, she talked and talked and grew more and more attached to Mrs. Groensma.

She would likely never come out of the coma, and she had no one in the world to care for her. Therefore, the time came for her to be transferred to a nursing home where she would eventually die. When Hanneke objected, she was heavily reprimanded for losing touch with her professional attitude and forbidden to contact the patient in the nursing home. Hanneke saw the logic of her supervisors but could not help thinking about Mrs. Groensma often.

Time went by, and Hanneke became a nurse and found a job in the Beatrix Hospital. One day at work, she was instructing a patient when a lady who was questioning another nurse turned and deliberately walked towards her. It was Mrs. Groensma! They found an empty room where they could speak privately, and Mrs. Groensma explained what she was doing there.

She recalled having been in a dark and lonely place, all alone, until the voice of what she thought must have been an angel started speaking, drawing her attention. Later when that voice stopped talking to her, she longed for the sound so much that she started struggling to get to the place where the voice had come from. She came out of the coma and took a long time to recover. Meanwhile she had questioned the nursing home staff. They eventually told her they had instructions to keep away a certain nurse who had made the mistake of getting too attached to her.

As soon as Mrs. Groensma was able, she came to the hospital to find that nurse. When she heard Hanneke talk to the patient, she recognized the voice that had spoken to her during her coma.

Mrs. Groensma took Hanneke's hand. "I have something I want to give you to thank you. I found it fifteen years ago in a ditch and originally wanted to put pictures of my late husband and me in it and give it to my daughter. When she died, I was all alone and wanted to throw it away, but I never got around to it. I now want you to have it."

Mrs. Groensma handed Hanneke a small box. Inside, sparkling

in the sunlight, lay a golden four-leaf-clover locket. With a pounding heart, Hanneke opened it to see her parents' photos.

Hanneke now wears the locket day and night and visits Mrs. Groensma whenever she wants.

And they talk and talk and grow more and more attached.

~Carin Klabbers
Chicken Soup for the Nurse's Soul

Abacus

To be upset over what you don't have is to waste what you do have.
~Ken S. Keyes, Jr., Handbook to Higher Consciousness

A lot has been written about what dogs can do for people. Dogs lead the blind, aid the deaf, sniff out illegal substances, give us therapeutic hope and joy, make us laugh with their idiosyncrasies, and give us companionship—to name just a few of their many talents. But what about our duty to dogs—what about their needs, wants, hopes and joys? And what about the ones most people do not want to adopt—the ones who aren't completely healthy or cute? This is a story of just such a dog.

I first learned about Abacus while doing some Internet research on special-needs dogs. I had become interested in special-needs dogs after losing my brother Damon, who was left paraplegic after an accident in 1992 and committed suicide three years later. Damon loved exploring the outdoors and preferred the freedom of driving a truck to working behind a desk all day. Losing those options was difficult enough for him, but the thought that nobody would want him was more than he could deal with. His death made me more aware of the challenges that people—and animals—with disabilities must face.

I knew my husband and I couldn't get a dog because of the no-pets policy at our rental, but I couldn't keep myself from researching them. On www.petfinder.com, there was a listing for a very handsome fellow named Abacus who was staying at Animal Lifeline, a no-kill animal shelter located near Des Moines, Iowa. Abacus had originally been rescued as a stray puppy two years earlier by the kind staff at a veterinary hospital in Nebraska after being hit by a car and subsequently paralyzed. Normally, a stray dog with partial paralysis would have been euthanized because few people want to adopt a dog in that condition. But the veterinarian and his staff saw something special and endearing in Abacus. They took him under their wing and eventually entrusted the shelter in Iowa with his care.

The picture of Abacus on the shelter's web site showed a largish black dog with a rubber ducky in a hydrotherapy tub, enjoying a workout to help improve the muscle tone in his paralyzed hind legs. Through his photograph alone, Abacus cast his spell on me and I was never the same.

I couldn't get the image of Abacus out of my mind and felt compelled to visit him—even though I knew I couldn't adopt him. My husband, John, supportive and understanding as always, drove with me on the nearly two-hour drive to the special-needs animal shelter. When I first saw Abacus in his quarters at the shelter, my breath stopped for a few seconds. It was a little disconcerting to see his atrophied hind legs, the result of his paralysis, but his exuberance and happy-go-lucky attitude quickly masked his physical challenges. I was struck by the sheer joy he radiated. His wide, loving eyes stayed in my mind and heart long after we drove away from the shelter.

Meeting Abacus inspired me to start looking for a house to buy instead of continuing to rent. Soon we found a nice rural home with acreage at an affordable price. I applied to adopt Abacus, and we were able to celebrate his third birthday by bringing him home with us a few weeks later.

Life with Abacus required a few adjustments. I learned daily therapeutic exercises for his hind legs, and how to get his strong, wiggly body into his wheelchair (called a K-9 cart) by myself. His castle, when I am not home, is a special padded room with a comfy mattress and lots of blankets and washable rugs. Often, I wrap his paralyzed legs in gauze bandages to help protect them from the abrasions he gets from dragging them on the floor or from the uncontrollable muscle spasms that occur in his hindquarters.

When Abacus is inside the house but out of his cart, he scoots around using his strong, muscular front legs. At times he can support his hind legs for a while, which looks a bit like a donkey kicking and occasionally causes him to knock things down as he maneuvers around the house. But when he is in his K-9 cart, Abacus can run like the wind. We have to supervise our canine Evel Knievel in his cart, since he can tip it over and get stuck when taking curves too fast.

Even though he requires extra care, I have never thought of Abacus as a burden. Living with him is a privilege. Enthusiastic about everything, he treats strangers like long-lost friends. And as much as he loves food, he loves cuddles even more. His zest for life inspires me, as well as others who meet him. Some people who see him feel pity for his challenges, but I always point out that he is not depressed or daunted by his differentness. I am sure if Abacus could speak, he would say that special-needs dogs can live happy, full lives and can enrich the lives of their adopters as much as—if not more than—a "normal" dog can.

The main reason I adopted Abacus was because I wanted to give him the comfort and security of a forever home, but in addition to that, I felt that he could help me give encouragement to others. A principle I have always lived by was shaped by part of an Emily Dickinson poem I learned as a child:

> If I can ease one life the aching
> Or cool one pain,
> Or help one fainting robin
> Unto his nest again,
> I shall not live in vain.

I only wish my brother could have known Abacus. For although animal-assisted therapy is not a cure-all, I believe a seed of hope can be planted in the heart of a physically, mentally or emotionally challenged child—or adult—when he sees a special-needs animal living a full and happy life in a loving home.

To spread this hope, I worked with Abacus to train him to become a certified therapy dog. After passing an evaluation this year, Abacus has begun visiting a school for special children. My employers at Farm Sanctuary—an organization that understands the mutual healing power that people and animals share—graciously grant me permission to take time off work for these twice-monthly weekday visits. Abacus looks forward to these excursions and always wows the kids (and teachers) with his bouncy "Tigger-like" personality. On occasion, his visiting attire includes his snazzy Super Dog cape that flies behind him as he zooms around in his wheelchair. Abacus always leaves happiness in his wake.

Living with a special-needs animal isn't for everyone, but it is a rare treat for those who choose to take it on. In fact, my experience with Abacus has inspired me to adopt a number of other special-needs animals over the years. All of them have more than repaid my investment of time and energy by being constant positive reminders that life's challenges need not be met with despair and negativity. Their love is healing, their appreciation rewarding, and their quirky personalities add priceless meaning to my life.

~Meghan Beeby
Chicken Soup for the Dog Lover's Soul

You Don't Have to Wear a Thong to Belong!

A friend accepts us as we are yet helps us to be what we should.
~Author Unknown

In the winter of 1989, I was thirty-one years old and weighed over three hundred pounds. I spent my days on a couch in front of the TV and suffered every minute, barely able to move or even breathe. I had so much to offer—as a mom, as a wife, as a person—but I felt trapped in my miserable shell. More than anything in the world I wanted help, someone to believe in and to believe in me—a friend to take my hand.

That winter I met Ellen Langley, and my life began to change. She was ten years older and nearly as large, but was calm and self-assured. That fascinated me and drew me into what became a big sister-little sister relationship, a gift of precious friendship.

Because of our friendship, I took the first steps toward actually doing something about my body. It started with a Christmas present from Ellen: a month's membership at one of the hottest fitness clubs in Lake Charles.

"Don't worry," Ellen said as she steered me toward the plate-glass doors. "You're gonna be fine."

I wouldn't have done it if Ellen hadn't come with me. My two little boys had been shocked that morning when their mommy had actually turned off the TV and walked out the door wearing elephant-sized sweatpants and the biggest purple shirt I could find. Now I was amazed as we walked into a room filled with perfect bodies in thongs. Ellen strode in like she owned the place. I was speechless looking at her, as she acted like she was right at home and chatted comfortably with everybody. I, on the other hand, was miserable.

I had already tried the health club scene. Before I'd moved to Lake Charles, I was so lonely and so desperate to find a friendly face that I actually hauled myself to an aerobics studio and signed up for a class. I thought it would be the perfect place to find a friend, but from the minute I slunk into that workout room, the students and instructor alike edged away and averted their eyes. I was so ashamed of my size. I did what I could to keep up, shuffling my feet a little bit and praying for a break, hoping someone would at least say hi.

I had given it my best shot for over a year, only lost a few pounds and was still lonely and ignored. I retreated to food, my source of comfort, love and security. It pushed me past the magic 300-pound mark; it nailed me to the sofa twelve hours a day because I had the lung capacity of a chipmunk. I couldn't even get up to play with my little boys, who had learned not to even bother asking. My emotional fuse was so short that I was snapping at my husband, Keith, and the boys.

Still, there I was at an aerobics studio trying it again. Once the workout began, things got worse. My self-consciousness was displaced by utter despair. The warm-up alone almost killed me. Everyone had their arms up over their heads, stretching, yet I couldn't lift mine past my shoulders. They all bent to touch their toes. I couldn't even see my toes. Then the actual class began — and I just couldn't do it. Two or three minutes of faking it, tapping my toes or whatever, and I had to stop. I felt like a freak. Why was I subjecting myself to this torture?

I looked over at Ellen's strength and told myself, No, you are not going to quit. You're going to stay here if it kills you. And it felt like it would. It felt that way for a long time. I learned to ignore the smirks, sideways glances and looks of pity. The first six months it was Ellen's presence and attitude that kept me going. We had to drive thirty miles each way to the classes, and sometimes we'd just sit in the car before class, having what we called "mini-therapy sessions."

One day, the owner of the club greeted me by name. "Hi, Dee," she said. It was as if the heavens had opened. Words can't describe what that did for my self-esteem. Here was a woman who was tall, thin as a rail, had zero percent body fat and a resting heart rate of 42. And she knew my name.

I made that dinky little "Hi" into a mountain of self-esteem, something I could cling to until another crumb came my way. And they kept coming, those crumbs. A growing number of my classmates began treating me like I belonged, once I showed them I was there to stay. Instructors adjusted my movements to fit the restrictions of my body, and in my own way I began to bloom.

By the end of 1990, I was disappointed that I'd only lost thirty pounds, a mere sliver from my beginning weight of over 300. While it didn't seem like much, I could now do things I hadn't done in years. My mood and energy improved, and I was off the couch. I even ventured outside to play with the boys. I wasn't biting my husband's head off, and I could visit friends, shop, work out and just live.

My eating habits were different; I could stop when full and there were no more midnight refrigerator raids. I learned to enjoy the taste of the food now that I wasn't cramming it in, and I didn't lie about the cookies I ate because I wasn't eating the whole package. The change was happening gradually, naturally. I wasn't super diligent. The place I did my pushing was in the aerobics room, and I let the rest take care of itself.

That aerobics room! Just showing up was a lifesaver. The music, the energy and Ellen—my oasis, the bright spot. Sometimes I'd run out of gas and just stop, wait a while, and then jump back in when I was ready. Sure I felt frustrated, self-conscious and intimidated. Sure I got a little pissed off sometimes. But I persisted... and that made all the difference in the world.

Then all the good fell away when, caught up in the Christmas rush, I stopped working out for three weeks. I regressed, started stuffing myself again, got cranky, began complaining. Finally, my husband even told me to get lost. "You're a nightmare," he said. He was right. I had slipped badly. I realized that my workout wasn't for my body or appearance or how others felt about me. My workout was for how I felt about myself, for how happy I was and how happy that made the people around me, the people I loved. I returned to the club in January with a vengeance. I thought every day about how my life was changing and about how others could be changed.

I thought to myself, How many other heavyweights would want to work out at a hard-body studio if they knew they'd be accepted and not too critically compared with the workout animals around them? How I would have loved people to give me the time of day or feel the instructors reach out. And then I thought, Why not me?

The next day I showed up at the studio to ask the owner: "Why can't I be an instructor?" Her reaction was predictable: partly supportive, partly disbelieving.

She said, "Neat idea, Dee." I actually heard in her tone, Gee, you might be onto something. Some of the staff, however, thought it was beyond ridiculous.

No matter. I enrolled in a National Dance-Exercise Instructor's Training Association (NDEITA) workshop, which included a written exam. The day of the test, I arrived at the Lake Charles YMCA, one of about thirty men and women.

No one was near my size and, of course, I got the usual "good for you, honey" looks. The daylong exam was a snap, and the next morning I was at the owner's office door with a perfect score.

"All right," I said. "Let's go."

She couldn't believe it. Tossing it back in my court, she told me if I could get ten people to sign up for a month, she'd give me a room and a time slot.

So I made up my own flyers and taped them up at every Weight Watchers location, plus-size clothing shop and grocery store in town. They introduced a brand-new, very-low-intensity pre-aerobics workout specifically for overweight people, taught by an overweight instructor.

Twelve prospects signed up—all women. And so, on a Monday morning in April 1991, I walked into the studio and for the first time stepped to the front of the class.

I could see the owner and the staff watching, getting a load of the misfits. I said a silent prayer, popped my tape into the machine, punched the "Play" button... and... kicked... aerobic... butt.

It was like magic. It felt so good to be in front of that class, motivating them, helping them feel accepted, comfortable, like they belonged—because they did. I watched their faces light up and laugh as they moved. It was the most memorable hour of my life, that first class—the hour went by like a minute. It was incredible.

Beyond the inspiration and identification, I gave everyone specialized attention the second she came through that door, assessing her abilities and adjusting techniques to meet her limitations. No one in that room was going to have to bail out and just watch.

Three years after teaching my first class I was awarded Nike's Fitness Innovation Award for the program I created. The New Face of Fitness has been implemented nationally into more than thirty YWCAs through a Nike grant. It has expanded into hospitals, corporations and fitness clubs across the country.

I weigh about 220 pounds and have maintained my hundred-pound loss for years now. I have regular checkups that confirm I've corrected my medical problems, including high blood pressure, elevated blood cholesterol and diabetes.

With all my newfound energy I even wrote a book—*Thin Is Just a Four-Letter Word: Living Fit for All Shapes and Sizes*—that sold far beyond anyone's wildest dreams.

The last thing on my mind fourteen years ago when Ellen helped me find the courage to walk through those doors was that I could actually teach aerobics classes, much less write a book, work on my own video series, and sign up with an agent who negotiated several sports equipment endorsements for me.

The truth is I wouldn't be here if my students hadn't seen a woman their own size in front of those mirrors. They told me so. If I could do that, they said, then by God, so could they.

~Dee Hakala
Chicken Soup to Inspire the Body and Soul

Woman to Woman

True Friends

*A friend drops their plans when you're in trouble,
shares joy in your accomplishments, feels sad when you're in pain.
A friend encourages your dreams and offers advice—
but when you don't follow it, they still respect and love you.
~Doris W. Helmering*

The Golden Girls

A friend is one of the nicest things you can have,
and one of the best things you can be.
~Douglas Pagels

Rose and I met when we were in our mid-twenties. I had invited her daughter to my daughter's third birthday party, and Rose came along. We scrutinized each other and assessed the obvious differences. She was a smoker; I wasn't. I dressed conservatively; she didn't. She wore a long, black flowing wig whenever she tired of her short frosted hair; I wore the same "flip" hairstyle for years. But we became best friends.

Despite our differences, we wore a path from my house to hers (sometimes in our fuzzy robes), borrowing sugar, guzzling coffee, sharing baked goods and details of our lives. For twelve years, we went to yard sales, fast-food restaurants, playgrounds and school events together.

Rose and I stayed best friends during tough times, as well. Both of us had turbulent marriages. One summer, both marriages finally fell apart. Coincidentally, Rose's sister Millie ended her marriage about the same time, and so did Rose's childhood friend, Judy.

The four of us became known as The Golden Girls. We discovered a neighborhood club with an outdoor patio, and we spent that summer sipping soda and dancing together to old-time rock and roll.

After that summer, we calmed down a bit. As we created new lives for ourselves, we saw less of each other. Eventually, Rose and I attended each other's weddings, and we visited together at family gatherings and holiday celebrations. Each time, it was as if we'd never been apart.

At my daughter's baby shower, I noticed that Rose's one-of-a-kind laugh seemed hoarse. She told me she'd had a persistent cough for weeks. Soon, diagnostic tests indicated a mass in her lung. Exploratory surgery revealed a large inoperable malignancy. I visited Rose in the intensive care unit afterward.

"I love you," I told my friend, realizing it was the first time I had said the words aloud.

"I love you, too," she said groggily, sealing our bond.

After Rose recovered from surgery, I took her for radiation treatment. We held hands in the waiting room. When our eyes met, they brimmed with tears. On the drive home, we talked about this life and the afterlife. And we talked about a story we'd both read many, many years before, about two friends, one of whom was terminally ill.

"You'll remember that story, won't you?" Rose asked.

"I will," I promised.

The Golden Girls reunited. Millie, Judy and I spent countless hours with Rose. We took her shopping and dining. We humored her when her medication gave her hallucinations. When she became incapacitated, we visited her at home in shifts. I fluffed her pillows, brought her doughnuts, massaged her feet and colored in coloring books with her.

Rose spent the last week of her life in the hospital, heavily sedated, surrounded by loved ones. At fifty-one, her breathing ceased and our mourning began.

A year followed, and I thought of Rose often. One cold November morning, as I left for work, I saw something pink protruding from a drift of decaying leaves. I cleared the debris and gasped in disbelief at a flower bud. During the summer I had planted a tiny, three-inch potted azalea, hoping it would grow into a bush. It hadn't grown at all and had never flowered. But here on this frosty Missouri morning, with the rest of the garden killed by a hard frost, the azalea bloomed.

I thought about Rose all day, and that afternoon, I called her daughter.

"Denise, can you come by after work?" I asked. "I have a surprise from your mom."

When I got home, I checked the azalea again. The tiny pink bud had opened completely and blossomed to the size of a carnation.

That evening, Denise came to my door. She looked just like Rose.

"You're not going to believe this," I said. I told Denise about the conversation Rose and I had had after her radiation therapy.

"Twenty years ago, your mom and I read a story about two best friends. One was terminally ill. She vowed to make a flower bloom in winter to prove there was an afterlife. Your mom and I discussed that story and made a pact that day."

I led Denise to the backyard and showed her my azalea, blooming in winter. Denise and I laughed, embraced, stared in disbelief and cried tears of joy.

"This couldn't have come at a better time," Denise said, wiping her eyes. "It's been almost a year since Mom passed away. You've taken away so much of my sadness. Thank you."

During the next week I watched in amazement as three more flowers bloomed fully. I called Millie and Judy and told them about the plant I nicknamed The Golden Girls, with one blossom for each of us. We rejoiced at the message from our friend. Incredibly, the plant thrived for two weeks, surviving snow, wind and chill. Then, the flowers gradually withered and died, completing the cycle of life. But they left behind a vivid memory and a message for all us Golden Girls that true friendship never dies.

~Linda O'Connell
Chicken Soup for the Gardener's Soul

Birthday Presents

Since there is nothing so well worth having as friends,
never lose a chance to make them.
~Francesco Guicciardini

I clicked my Palm Pilot and flashing words reminded me that I had not completed a task. Staring at the screen, I worried about what in the world I was going to get Colette for her birthday. After almost thirty years of friendship, I was running out of ideas. And it wasn't just for Colette.

I was blessed to have seven incredible lifelong friendships that began in my childhood. Colette, Marcy, Amy and I became steadfast friends while coloring in kindergarten. We added Mary, Kimmie and Rachel to the group in junior high while chasing boys. Claudette joined us in high school while going to football games. With friendships that spanned decades, together we played jump rope, studied, went to dances, fell in and out of love, graduated, traveled, began careers, really fell in love, married and had children. This colorful group of friends had seen each other at our very best and our very worst. No matter what changed in our lives, one thing stayed the same — our friendships.

Here I was, though, staring at my Palm Pilot realizing I was going to be really late with Colette's birthday gift if I did not buy her something today. What could I get her? Last year was a magazine subscription, the year before that candles, before that wineglasses, and before that scrapbook-making kits. Besides, as my friends married and we grew older, we already had just about everything we needed. What could I buy her?

The phone rang and I was happy to escape my unsuccessful pondering. Marcy greeted me cheerfully and began to tell me about last night's girls' dinner. Conversations like this always made me miss my childhood home in Illinois and made it hard to live in Washington, D.C., so far from my friends. Marcy filled me in on the latest gossip. Mary was pregnant with child number four and Amy's son Jake was potty-training. Colette would probably be engaged very soon and Marcy was finalizing her wedding plans. On and on we chatted while laughing about the latest happenings in our lives. Finally, I asked Marcy what she was giving Colette for her birthday. Marcy exclaimed, "Oh, I almost forgot to tell you! Last night we were all talking about our birthdays and how hard it is to buy something unique and useful after all these years of friendship. Also, with everyone having kids, school costs, homes, vacations and basically life, we decided that expensive birthday gifts for our friends really add up. So we decided that this year we're giving each other socks." I laughed and said, "What a great idea!" Marcy continued, "No more than two pairs and they can be any kind of socks. You know, those cute little socks with patterns, or trouser socks, or workout socks. Whatever you want. Next year we're all giving underwear! You should have heard that discussion about who wears thongs, granny underwear or lace! It was hilarious. The year after that we're giving earrings. Isn't this fun?" I quickly agreed and kept smiling. We chatted a few more minutes and hung up.

I tossed my Palm Pilot into my purse and headed to the store. While driving, I couldn't help but think about how smart my friends were. It wasn't the physical gift or the amount of money we spent that was important. What was important was celebrating our friends' birthdays. The inexpensive themes allowed us to be clever, and perhaps even funny, yet it would be low-stress and useful. As I thought of the years ahead, I smiled because from now on birthday buying was going to be so easy and fun. And when you really think about it, regardless of what's inside when we unwrap each other's presents, what we really unwrap is our love.

~Marguerite Murer
Chicken Soup for the Girlfriend's Soul

Loving Kelly

"I really like her," my brother told me over the phone.

"Well, tell me all about her," I said. Then I asked all those nosy questions only a sister can get away with asking. What's she like? Where did you meet? Is she "the one?"

I could hear the smile in his voice as he told me about her, and in my mind, I could see that familiar glint in his eyes. For the next twenty minutes, Steve told me all about his new girlfriend. As I continued to listen, I began to know something was not quite right. Then I realized he had not yet told me her name.

"What's her name?" I finally asked, trying to sound lighthearted.

Seconds of silence stretched into an eternity before he quietly, hesitantly, said, "Kelly."

Suddenly, the phone seemed to grow hot in my trembling hand, and I could not speak. Finally, with some effort, I said, "Oh." Then, "I gotta go. I'll call you soon." I sat there for a long time, staring at the phone, remembering another Kelly.

I still remember the first time I saw her. I was seven. I came crashing into the house after school only to be met by the shushing sound escaping around my mother's index finger held firmly against her pursed lips. "Quiet. The baby's sleeping," she whispered.

"Can I see her?" I whispered back, stepping up onto my tiptoes.

"When she wakes up," Mom said firmly.

I looked at Dad. I knew he would help me.

He winked and motioned me over. Ignoring Mom's warning, we sneaked into my bedroom where Kelly, wearing a tiny cornflower-blue gown, lay sleeping. I pressed my face against the rails of her crib. I reached between the bars and touched her cheek. Dad knelt beside me and gently woke her. Kelly opened her blue eyes and looked right into mine.

"My sister, my baby sister," I said in a proud sigh. I loved her from that moment on.

As we grew older and more aware of life, we giggled about boys, and clothes and hairstyles. I answered her questions about periods and love and falling stars. We crossed our hearts and hoped to die should we ever not be best friends.

At night, as we lay in bed with our backs pressed against each other, we shared all our secrets and all our dreams and carefully planned our old age. We would live together and travel the world. We would be "fun old ladies" like the Baldwin Sisters from Walton's Mountain.

When the day came for me to leave for college, Kelly and I clung to each other, and we sobbed into each other's necks for a long time. With Kelly still weeping softly, Mom finally pulled her away and assured me she would be okay. I wasn't sure I would be, though.

When I was twenty-five and Kelly was eighteen, my doctor diagnosed me with a serious illness that left me unable to bear children. Kelly came to me and offered herself as a surrogate to carry a baby for me and my husband, Jeff.

I thought about her offer for a long time. I was more touched than words can say, but not at all surprised. In the end, I decided against it. I loved Kelly so much. I could not, would not, ask her to carry a baby in my stead then give it up to me, even though I knew she would. If only I could have known then what lay ahead just a year later.

Funny, isn't it, how you know when the phone rings it's bad news. It was January 26, 1986, Sunday afternoon, Super Bowl Sunday. We had hamburgers for lunch.

"Yes. When? I see," Jeff said into the phone.

There was no hiding it. I saw the shadow in his eyes. "It's bad, isn't it?" I asked as Jeff slowly replaced the receiver in its cradle.

He held me tightly and gently broke the news. "It's Kelly. She's dead. It seems that carbon monoxide seeped through a crack in an old heater in the hotel room where she was staying last night. She died in her sleep."

My sister, my baby sister. Gone! I couldn't believe it. We had so many plans. It just couldn't be true. It just couldn't.

Three years after Kelly's death, I still found it difficult to talk about her. I could not even speak her name without tears filling my eyes. The thought of Steve dating and possibly marrying someone named Kelly was almost unbearable.

Steve did marry "his Kelly," and I found myriad ways to speak of her without actually saying her name. To Steve — How's your wife? How's she doing? To Mom and Dad — Have you heard from Steve and his wife — from them — from her?

With Steve and Kelly living in Washington, D.C., Jeff and I by then in Alaska, and the lack of travel funds, I did not meet Steve's Kelly until six years after she married him. I did talk with her occasionally on the phone.

She seemed nice, and my brother was certainly happy. I began to look forward to her phone calls but still found myself holding back.

Then, one Christmas everything changed. Steve and Kelly and Jeff and I met at my parents' home in Texas. Kelly and I spent a lot of time talking and really getting to know each other. In spite of my reticence, I found myself liking her more and more. We laughed and giggled and shared secrets, almost like sisters.

"I've always wondered something," Kelly said as we walked through my parents' neighborhood one afternoon.

"What's that?" I asked.

"I wonder if your Kelly would have liked me."

Surprising myself, I answered immediately without hesitating. "Oh, I know she would. She would have scrutinized you closely, but she definitely would have liked you," I said knowingly. "You are beautiful, sweet, adventurous and fun. You like cats. And, most of all, you make her brother happy. And she would have loved your name."

On Christmas Eve, with tears dancing in her eyes, Kelly handed me a small beige and dark green box tied with twine. I pulled the free end of the string and lifted the lid. I gently removed the top layer of cotton. Underneath was a small magnet. Pink and purple pansies surrounded carefully chosen words: "Sisters By Marriage, Friends By Heart."

Tears escaped my control and wetted my cheeks. "Thank you, Kelly," I whispered. Then, I hugged her. "I love you."

Several Christmases have come and gone since that one. Kelly has become one of my very best friends, and another sister whom I love very much. The magnet she gave me still hangs on my refrigerator so that I will see it every day and be reminded of the love we share, that I almost never knew.

~Pamela Haskin
Chicken Soup for the Sister's Soul

Ladies of the Garden Club

Let us be grateful to people who make us happy;
they are the charming gardeners who make our souls blossom.
~Marcel Proust

"Me? Join a garden club?" I asked my boss in amazement. "Why in the world would I do that?"

I was a career-oriented woman in my early thirties. I had no time for a garden. And unless it was a business networking group, I had no interest in clubs.

"As employees of the community health department, our mission is to make the city a healthier place to live," Mrs. Hubbard informed me. I had no idea how joining a garden club would accomplish that. And I had no idea that Mrs. Hubbard's mother was the club president. All I knew was, the boss said "Go"—so I went.

My first meeting was on a Wednesday morning. Looking for the address, I was captivated by the beautiful gardens in this historic Oklahoma City neighborhood. Mature trees formed a canopy blocking the sun's glare, while vibrant purple irises, red and yellow tulips and a sea of white pansies illuminated the yard at Dorothy's home. What a contrast to my new house in the suburbs, where the front flower bed was filled with nothing but pine bark.

Though I was a few minutes late for the meeting, only three others had arrived. The dining room table was set for a full breakfast of quiche, fruit, sausage balls, and poppy seed and banana-nut muffins.

Members slowly trickled in. I was on my third cup of coffee, yet the meeting had not begun. I was a little edgy from the caffeine rush and the thought of all I needed to do at work. Then I learned that the meeting ended at noon and the ladies usually went out to lunch together afterward. I greeted that news with a smile and clenched teeth, and tried to keep from drumming my fingers impatiently.

The members, all past retirement age, introduced themselves. I was the only young person there. But as the meeting began, I found myself relaxing, captivated by the program on native plant species. I was so engrossed in imagining my own bare lawn bursting with plants, that I was caught off guard when President Bonnie announced, "We'd like to hold the meeting at your house next month, Stephanie — if you don't mind."

At the office later that day, I complained to a coworker. "The last thing I want to do is host a dozen women my grandmother's age," I groaned. "The meeting took all morning. And then they wanted me to go out to lunch! I'd been with them two hours already!" But I was stuck.

A month later, on a Wednesday morning, I dashed around my little kitchen. I dumped frozen mini-quiches from a sack and arranged them on a cookie sheet. I whacked two cans of quick-bake cinnamon rolls on the edge of the counter and slapped the doughy blobs on another pan.

This meeting will not be like the last, I thought grimly, looking at my store-bought refreshments. They probably wanted young people in the club just to do all the work!

The doorbell rang.

"I'm a little early, but I thought you could use some help getting ready for your first meeting," announced Dorothy as she entered. "I know you're a busy career gal, so I prepared a casserole and a fruit plate."

Entering the kitchen, she offered to make coffee as I tried to hide evidence of the Pillsbury Doughboy.

"Oh, good! Those cinnamon rolls are my favorites," she confided.

The doorbell rang again. Dorothy suggested she greet members so I could concentrate on being the hostess.

Soon, more than a dozen ladies were assembled. The meeting ran smoothly, and everyone seemed to enjoy the refreshments—even the ones from the frozen-food section.

"Now, since you've been our hostess today, we have a gift for you," said Bonnie. "Open your front door."

When I did, my jaw dropped in surprise. A dozen sacks filled with homegrown plants, potted shrubs and a flat of pansies welcomed me.

"It's your initiation," said Bonnie, laughing heartily. "We brought you something from our own gardens with a note on where to plant it and how to care for it."

"I brought the pansies," whispered Dorothy. "I noticed you admired them at our meeting last month."

Tears blurred my eyes as I thanked them. "I was embarrassed for you all to come out here. My yard is so bare."

"Oh my, no!" exclaimed Bonnie. "It's just a blank canvas waiting for an artist's brush."

Most everyone stayed to help me wash dishes and rearrange chairs.

Two days later, I got a call from Bonnie. "I've separated some coreopsis to plant around your fence," she said. "Say, if you haven't put the plants from Wednesday in the ground, I'll come Saturday morning and help if you want me to. You have been watering them daily, right?"

"Of course," I lied.

That evening I went home and tended the wilting plants, hoping they would revive overnight before Bonnie's arrival.

At seven in the morning, shovels in hand, three members of the Carefree Rose Garden Club arrived. They taught me how to arrange my landscape, and we dug a new twenty-foot flower bed around my front yard. The ladies brought more irises, amaryllis, tulips, hyacinths, coreopsis, pansies, peonies, redbud trees, wisteria, daisies and crepe myrtle bushes. We finished before noon, exhausted.

"It's beautiful," I whooped, as we brushed clumps of dirt and leaves off one another. "I could never have done it without you."

"That's garden club," said Bonnie.

We all staggered over to wash up at the garden hose. Then Dorothy asked me to get a picnic basket and ice chest from her car.

"I thought we'd be too tired to fix lunch, so I made us sandwiches before I came," she said.

Sitting cross-legged on the sidewalk with my newfound elderly friends, I realized I had never been muddier in my adult life. And, I giggled to myself, I couldn't remember having this much fun.

Me? Join a garden club? Where do I sign up?

~Stephanie Welcher Buckley
Chicken Soup for the Gardener's Soul

Got Tea?

Generosity lies less in giving much than in giving at the right moment.
~Jean La Bruyere

I've known Jenny since the day I started taking piano lessons from her mother. Jenny is blond; I am brunette. All-American Jenny is tall and vivacious. I am petite and quiet. Jenny has a bubbling troupe of siblings; I am an only child. Her favorite flavor is vanilla; I prefer chocolate. Jenny took piano lessons because it was what girls did when they were young, whereas I made music my life.

Our favorite pastime back then was our afternoon tea parties. My first tea set was a Christmas gift the year I was seven. The miniature pieces were decorated with garlands of pink roses and delicate violets. The tea set was accompanied by a charming old trunk filled with all manner of dress-up clothes Mother discovered at the secondhand store. Jenny and I rummaged through the trunk, combining fancy hats, strings of pearls and ecru sweaters with gold buttons until we were pleased with our queenly appearance. We would sit across my child-size table, sipping apple juice and nibbling crackers from the tiny dishes.

Under the Christmas tree every year was a package for the dress-up trunk. Favorite items were kept in the royal collection; others were replaced with new fashion trends. When we were ten, Jenny and I styled each other's hair before foraging through the trunk for high-heeled shoes. With wobbling ankles, we made our way precariously to the kitchen table to pour hot cocoa from Mother's teapot into adult-size mugs, and sample chocolate-chip cookies. And always we talked about our hopes, our dreams and our music.

At thirteen, Jenny and I painted our fingernails with polish and our faces with makeup from the trunk. With a drop of perfume behind each ear, we imagined ourselves as Abigail Adams and Martha Washington discussing the fledgling United States of America, or authors Beatrix Potter and Louisa May Alcott debating book ideas.

For our sixteenth birthdays, Jenny and I pierced our ears. The old trunk held an assortment of brash, dangly earrings we would not wear in public, but which were entirely suitable for tea. Linen napkins across our laps, we savored real tea from Mother's real china tea set, enhanced by slices of banana bread. We made plans to see the world. I would be her bridesmaid, and she promised to be mine.

Eighteen found us on the college rollercoaster. High school graduation flung us at whirlwind speed into the adult world of studies and jobs, cars and insurance, fellows and romance. Jenny's life went one way, mine another. On that vast university campus in fast-paced Southern California, we rarely saw one another.

Except for one special day. We ran into each other on campus and discovered we both had thirty minutes before we needed to be somewhere else. With sudden lightheartedness, we dashed to the nearby café for tea... orange spice for Jenny, raspberry for me. There was so much to talk about. Jenny had met a man with hair as dark as hers was blond. Work at the art gallery and art studies consumed the rest of her time. I was simultaneously pursuing two doctoral degrees in music and squeezing in a few hours of work. And there was a man in my life.

Those precious free minutes turned into a stolen four hours, and we realized with a start that afternoon classes had long since ended. But sitting on the table between us was a teapot our intuitive waitress had discreetly set there before she left to carry on her life away from the café. The bill read, "On the house."

I married that special man in my life. As promised, Jenny was my bridesmaid. My husband and I set up housekeeping in a vintage house near the college, close to family and friends and all that was dear to me. Jenny and I fit in an occasional cup of tea.

Then everything changed. My husband landed an excellent job with a promising future, great benefits and good salary, all in the field he wanted. He was elated. He said, "The move five hundred miles north would be a terrific adventure."

Adventure? I was devastated. All I knew and was familiar with was here. I needed six more months to complete my studies. I didn't know a soul in the new town so far away. I wasn't one who made friends easily. What would I do there?

Moving so far from loved ones proved extremely difficult. I spent the first days crying as I unpacked boxes in our beautiful new home. Everything felt, and looked, gray.

Then came the first knock on my new door. Standing on the front porch was the mailman with a large parcel. I recognized the return address as Jenny's. Dear, lifelong friend Jenny. Those horrible miles between us melted away, as I tore at the wrapping.

The paper parted to reveal a teapot, decorated with garlands of pink roses and delicate violets. Nestled next to the beautiful china piece was a matching set of teacups and saucers along with a box of raspberry tea. Her note read: "I know you will need a close friend in your new home. You have my permission to find a new close friend. Then you will have two close friends."

Sunday, my husband and I visited the nearby church. Renee, an effervescent lady with auburn hair, gave me a hug. "We moved here a year ago, and I know just how lonely you feel."

"Would you come for tea?" I asked.

"I'd be delighted," Renee said with a smile.

Months later, Jenny sent a smaller package, a box of orange spice tea. The enclosed note read, "I'll be there Saturday for tea!" And so Jenny made her first of many visits to our northern home.

When I called Jenny with the news I was expecting our first baby, she sent a package of peppermint tea, to soothe my nauseous tummy.

It's been fifteen years since my husband and I moved north.

Renee brought me a beribboned package containing a mug with the picture of an angel and the words, "May your guardian angel keep watch over you when we're apart." Renee and her family were moving out of state.

I sent Renee off with a hug and a package to open on the drive to their new address. The gift bag held a pair of teacups and a note that read: "You will need a close friend in your new home. You have my permission to find one. Then you will have two close friends."

Jenny and I keep in touch mostly by phone. As always, we are startlingly different. Jenny's life takes her to exciting and glamorous places. My world is filled with my three children, carpooling, church and music.

Just last week, Jenny telephoned.

"How wonderful to hear from you," I exclaimed. "But I'm in the middle of giving a piano lesson. Can I call you back?"

"I'm afraid not," she replied with a laugh. "I'm calling from a layover in a New York airport. I'm putting a package in the mail, some delicious herbal teas from a little shop. I thought of you immediately. It's some of those berry flavors you adore...."

~PeggySue Wells
Chicken Soup for the Girlfriend's Soul

Woman to Woman

Special Moments

Love the moment,
and the energy of that moment will spread beyond all boundaries.
~Sister Corita Kent

Lunch with Helen Keller

My husband and I loved our house in Italy. It sat high on a cliff above Portofino with an extraordinary view of the blue harbor below, and its white beach was surrounded by cypresses. There was, however, a serpent in our paradise: the path up the cliff. The municipal authorities refused to grant us permission to build a proper road in lieu of the mule track. The only vehicle that could climb the narrow path and negotiate the hairpin turns, the steep incline and the potholes, was an old American Army Jeep we had bought in Genoa. It possessed neither springs nor brakes. When you wanted to stop, you had to go into reverse and back up against something. But it was indestructible, and you could rely on it in all weathers.

One day in the summer of 1950, our neighbor, Contessa Margot Besozzi, who of necessity also owned a Jeep, called to say that her cousin had arrived in town with a companion and that her own Jeep had conked out. Would I mind going to fetch the two old ladies in ours? They were at the Hotel Splendido.

"Whom should I ask for at the hotel?" I asked.

"Miss Helen Keller."

"Who?"

"Miss Helen Keller, K-e-l-l...."

"Margot, you don't mean Helen Keller?"

"Of course," she said. "She's my cousin. Didn't you know?"

I ran into the garage, jumped into the Jeep and raced down the mountain.

I had been twelve years old when my father gave me the book about Helen Keller written by Anne Sullivan, the remarkable woman whom fate had chosen to be the teacher of the blind and deaf child. Anne Sullivan had turned the rebellious, brutish little child into a civilized member of society by teaching her to speak. I still remembered vividly her description of the first few months of physical battle with the child, until the glorious moment when she held Helen's left hand under a running water tap and the blind, deaf and up until then mute little girl made history by stammering out an intelligible word:

"Wa-ter."

Over the years I had read about Helen Keller in the newspapers. I knew that Anne Sullivan was no longer with her and that a new companion now accompanied her everywhere. But the few minutes it took me to drive down the hill were not nearly enough to get used to the idea that I was going to meet in person this mythical figure from my early youth.

I backed the Jeep up against a bougainvillea-covered wall and presented myself at the hotel. A tall, buxom, vigorous-looking woman rose from a chair on the hotel terrace to greet me: Polly Thomson, Helen Keller's companion. A second figure rose slowly from the chair beside her and held out her hand. Helen Keller, then in her seventies, was a slight, white-haired woman with wide-open blue eyes and a shy smile.

"How do you do?" she said slowly and a little gutturally.

I took her hand, which she was holding too high because she didn't know how tall I was. She was bound to make this mistake with people she was meeting for the first time, but she never made it twice. Later, when we said goodbye, she put her hand firmly into mine at exactly the right level.

The luggage was loaded into the back of the Jeep, and I helped the jolly Miss Thomson to sit beside it. The hotel porter lifted Helen Keller's fragile body and set it down on the front seat next to me. Only then did it dawn on me that this was going to be a risky undertaking.

The Jeep was open; there was nothing you could hold onto properly. How was I to keep the blind and deaf woman from falling out of the rickety old thing when we took a curve, which had to be done at a fast clip because of the angle and the Jeep's general condition? I turned to her and said, "Miss Keller, I must prepare you—we're going up a very steep hill. Can you hold tight to this piece of metal on the windshield?"

But she continued to look expectantly straight ahead. Behind me, Miss Thomson said patiently, "She can't hear you, dear, nor see you. I know it's hard to get used to it at first."

I was so embarrassed that I stammered like an idiot, trying to explain the problem ahead of us. All the while, Miss Keller never turned her head or seemed puzzled by the delay. She sat motionless, a slight smile on her face, patiently waiting. Miss Thomson knelt across the luggage and reached for her hand. Rapidly she moved Helen's fingers up, down and sideways, telling her in blind-deaf language what I had just said.

"I don't mind," said Helen, laughing. "I'll hold tight."

I took courage, got hold of her hands, and placed them on the piece of metal in front of her. "Okay," she cried gaily, and I switched on the ignition. The Jeep started with a jump and Miss Thomson fell off her seat on top of the luggage. I couldn't stop and help her up because of the steep hill, the dangerous curve ahead and the absence of brakes. We roared upward, my eyes glued to the narrow path, and Miss Thomson helpless as a beetle on its back.

I'd had plenty of passengers in the Jeep, and they'd all complained about the lack of springs. No wonder, with all those boulders and potholes, not to mention the hairpin turns through the olive trees, which only partially obscured the precipitous drop that had unnerved quite a few of our guests. Helen was the first passenger who was oblivious to the danger; she was enchanted by the violent jumps and only laughed when she was thrown against my shoulder. Helen actually began to sing. "This is fun," she warbled happily, bouncing up and down. "Lovely!" she cried.

We tore past our house at breakneck speed—out of the corner

of my eye I saw our gardener, Giuseppe, crossing himself—and continued onward and upward. I had no idea how Miss Thomson was doing, for the Jeep's fearful roar had long ago drowned out her anguished protests. But I knew that Helen was still next to me. Her thin white hair had come undone and fluttered about her face, and she was enjoying the crazy ride like a child riding up and down on a wooden horse on a merry-go-round.

At last we rounded the last curve between two giant fig trees, and I could see Margot and her husband waiting for us at their entrance gate. Helen was lifted out of the Jeep and hugged; the luggage was unloaded, and Miss Thomson upended and dusted off.

I was invited to lunch. While the two old ladies were being shown to their rooms to freshen up, Margot told me about her cousin and her life. Helen was famous the world over, and in every civilized country, the great and the renowned were eager to meet her and do something for her. Heads of state, scholars and artists vied to receive her, and she had traveled all over the world to satisfy her burning curiosity.

"But don't forget," said Margot, "all she really notices is a change of smell. Whether she's here or in New York or in India, she sits in a black, silent hole."

Arm in arm, casually, as if they just happened to be fond of each other, the two old ladies walked through the garden toward the terrace, where we were waiting for them.

"That must be wisteria," said Helen, "and masses of it, too. I recognize the scent."

I went to pick a large bunch of the blossoms, which surrounded the terrace, and laid it in her lap. "I knew it!" she cried happily, touching them.

Of course, Helen's diction was not quite normal. She spoke haltingly, like someone who has had a stroke, and her consonants were slow and labored. She turned to me, looking directly at me because she had sensed where I was sitting. "You know, we're on the way to Florence to see Michelangelo's David. I'm so thrilled; I've always wanted to see it."

Mystified, I looked at Miss Thomson, who nodded.

"It's true," she said. "The Italian government has had a scaffolding erected around the statue so that Helen can climb up and touch it. That's what she calls 'seeing.' We often go to the theater in New York, and I tell her what's going on onstage and describe the actors. Sometimes we go backstage, too, so that she can 'see' the sets and the actors. Then she goes home, feeling that she's really witnessed the performance."

All the time we were talking, Helen sat and waited. Now and then, when our conversation went on too long, I saw her thin fingers take her friend's hand inquiringly, never impatiently.

Luncheon was served on the terrace. Helen was led to her chair, and I watched her "see" her place setting. Quick as lightning, her hands moved over the objects on the table—plate, glass, silverware—memorizing where they were. Never once during the meal did she grope about; she reached out casually and firmly like the rest of us.

After lunch, we stayed on the shady terrace, surrounded by trailing clusters of wisteria like a thick mauve curtain, the sun below us glittering on the sea. Helen sat in the usual way, head raised slightly as though listening to something, her sightless blue eyes wide open. Her face, although an old lady's face, had something of a schoolgirl's innocence. Whatever suffering must have tormented her—and might still torment her, for all I knew—her face showed no trace of it. It was an isolated face, a saintly face.

I asked her, through her friend, what else she wanted to see in Italy. Then she slowly mapped out her Italian journey—all the places she wanted to visit and the people she would meet. Incredibly, she spoke French quite well and could make herself understood in German and Italian. Sculpture was, naturally, her favorite form of art, because she could touch it and experience it firsthand.

"There's still so much I'd like to see," she said, "so much to learn. And death is just around the corner. Not that that worries me. On the contrary."

"Do you believe in life after death?" I asked.

"Most certainly," she said emphatically. "It is no more than passing from one room into another."

We sat in silence.

Suddenly, Helen spoke again. Slowly and very distinctly she said, "But there's a difference for me, you know. Because in that other room, I shall be able to see."

~Lilli Palmer
A Second Chicken Soup for the Woman's Soul

13

My Blue-Eyed Boy

The soul is the same in all living creatures,
although the body of each is different.
~Hippocrates

My dog, Harry, and I are very close. Harry, an eighty-pound Dalmatian, listens to me when I am upset, comforts me when I am blue and goes everywhere with me. He cares for no other person like he does for me, his beloved mama. Having raised him since he was an eight-week-old pup, I feel the same way about him — he is my blue-eyed boy.

One beautiful Sunday morning, Harry and I went to Central Park. Harry was running off leash on Dog Hill, along with all the other city dogs, while their owners enjoyed a spring day in the park.

I was feeling down because I had been recently laid off from the job I'd held for ten years. Being in the park with Harry was one of the ways I forgot for a while that I was out of work — and that my prospects were not looking good in a tough economy.

I was standing at the bottom of Dog Hill talking to another dog owner, when all of a sudden, we heard someone shout, "He peed on my leg!" I turned to look, and, lo and behold, at the top of the hill I saw a lady gesticulating at my beloved boy, who apparently was the culprit. Horrified, I rushed up the hill. Harry had never done anything remotely like this before.

When I got to where the woman was standing, I reached down

quickly and grabbed hold of Harry's collar in case he decided to do anything else untoward. The woman was bent over, trying to clean up her leg. She was pulling off her shoe because the pee had dribbled down her leg all the way into her shoe.

We straightened up at the same moment, and for a shocked instant, we looked at each other.

"Alexandra!" she said.

"Valerie!" It was my former boss—the one who laid me off three months before.

I apologized to Valerie for Harry's behavior, but all the way home, I laughed and laughed, and gave Harry lots of kisses and hugs. Harry, of course, was thrilled that he clearly had pulled off a winning stunt—though, fortunately, he has never repeated his performance. To this day, when I think about all of Harry's wonderful qualities, his "revenge for mama" still makes me laugh the hardest.

~Alexandra Mandis
Chicken Soup for the Dog Lover's Soul

14

The Rose Babies

Just living is not enough.
One must have sunshine, freedom, and a little flower.
~Hans Christian Anderson

Most people press a flower in a book when they wish to keep it as a memento. My mother doesn't believe in preserving a memory by hiding it. Her motto is, "Don't press it! When will you look at it again tucked away in a book? Make it grow! Enjoy its beauty as a living flower, not as a withered keepsake."

That's my mother. She can make anything grow.

Recently, Mom received a mixed bouquet of flowers from her sister for her birthday. She is especially fond of roses and was delighted to find two roses in the bouquet. "Oh, look at the lovely roses. I've never seen such a beautiful shade of peach in a rose. I must save it as a souvenir."

I have seen this process many times, but I watch in awe each time. She takes one of the roses and cuts the bottom at an angle with a pair of scissors, wraps the bottom in a dampened paper towel and places the rose in a plastic bag to keep it moist.

Now I know it's my turn. The magic is about to begin. I run to the pantry to get a quart jar, once used for canning peaches.

"Here's the enchanted glass jar," I announce, as I return with it.

We head for her lilac bush. I carry the jar and the plastic bag that contains the rose. She carries warm water in an old coffee can, bent so that it has a spout on each side of it. My mother deliberately keeps her lilac bush overgrown. She trims it in such a way that it becomes fat and dense. The soil beneath it is damp and warm. She easily digs a hole with her hands and places the rose cutting in the hole. I help her carefully pack the dirt around the rose. She places the glass jar over the rose, and firmly twists it into the ground.

Finally, she gives the rose a drink, pointing the spout of the coffee can to the bottom of the glass jar. She whispers, "Oh, little rose, let me warm your toes, this'll keep you safe when the cold wind blows. See you in the spring, little rose."

"Little rose is all ready for her long winter's nap," she explains to me as we walk back to the house.

My mother is shameless when it comes to asking for a rose from someone's front yard or their garden. But no one ever refuses her request. And one time, the giver was especially glad she had shared her bounty.

It was a lovely summer day. My mother and I were walking past our neighbor Dorothy working in her garden. My mother stopped to admire one of Dorothy's roses.

"I've never seen such a beautiful lavender rose, blending into silver at the edge of the petals. Would you mind if I choose one to enjoy?" she asked Dorothy. Proud of her special lavender rosebush, Dorothy was delighted to cut the rose and graciously hand it to my mother. But the lavender rose did not go into a vase, as Dorothy probably assumed. It joined the others under the lilac bush, protected under its very own glass jar.

That Christmas, Dorothy told us that the beautiful lavender rosebush had been stricken by disease in the fall, and it couldn't be saved. "It was my favorite," she said sadly, "and I haven't been able to find another to replace it."

Spring was delayed that year, but finally the fear of frost was gone. My mother was eager to uncover her rose cuttings, each protected under its miniature greenhouse.

"I wonder how many of my rose babies will be ready to begin their new lives?" she mused.

As always, I watched in amazement as my mother uncovered her rose babies. Carefully, she twisted the first glass jar from the warm earth: It was the lavender rose clipping. Would that beautiful rose be reborn? She spied a baby shoot, a tiny leaf peeking its way through the stem. Indeed, the lavender rose was alive.

Mom whispered to me, "Wait until late summer, and I'll have a surprise for Dorothy. I'll nourish our baby, and it'll thrive into a beautiful bush. She'll have her lavender rosebush again. It'll be our secret until then."

And sure enough, late that summer, Dorothy cried for joy as she received her surprise—a healthy new lavender rosebush.

On the card was the following:

Here's a small gift from my garden to you.
It began the day someone gave me a rose, too.
I planted that rose in the good, warm earth,
And I nurtured it—hence its happy rebirth.
After you've planted this gift and it grows,
To keep up the cycle, may I impose?
If I may be bold, do you suppose,
That I might request its very first rose?

~Georgia A. Hubley
Chicken Soup for the Gardener's Soul

Taking It in Stride

Laughter is the closest thing to the grace of God.
~Karl Barth

As we grow older, life's embarrassing moments don't seem to send us into a tizzy like they did when we were seventeen. Remember how we used to fret and cry over the silliest things? Having a pimple at the end of our nose was a major crisis, charged with great drama and hysteria. Stumbling on the stairs during assembly was enough to keep us home for days, while eye contact with cute boys in the hall could easily send us bumping into walls. Nowadays, let's hope we can simply laugh about those little mishaps and chalk them up to experience.

Take, for example, what recently happened to me at a business conference in Salt Lake City. It's one of "those moments" that I'd like to forget but, unfortunately, is etched in my brain forever.

My flight arrived at the airport just thirty minutes before the first session in the afternoon. Luckily, the shuttle bus was at the curb and got me to the hotel in time to dash into the meeting room. I plopped my suitcase in the corner, grabbed my three-ring binder from it, and began mingling with other attendees as I found my way to a seat.

To my surprise and horror, the entire time I had been circulating around the room, a pair of my purple underpants was hooked onto the end of my notebook, clinging ever so nicely to my forearm for all to see. Let's just say

I'll never be a size two, and my undies aren't lacey little snippets from the Victoria's Secret catalog. No, I get my practical cotton underwear at Sears in the full-figure department next to lawn chairs and power tools.

As I approached the table and noticed my faux pas, my undies did additional damage by falling smack-dab into the teacup of the gentleman seated in the next chair. The weight and bulk of the fabric tipped the cup over, spilling hot water across the tablecloth onto the poor man's lap. What could I do but scoop the panties up and offer him another cup of tea? (I can't remember, but I hope I didn't wring them out — that would have been so tacky.) Meekly, he declined, but to his credit and courage, he stayed right there for the rest of the session, turning out to be a good sport about the entire fiasco.

Everyone had a good laugh, me included. If I had been seventeen, I would have had to drop out of school and move to another town, but at age forty-five I could laugh along with everyone else. What else could I do, especially when many at the conference asked about next year's encore? Perhaps I'll do something in pink!

~Cappy Tosetti
Chicken Soup to Inspire a Woman's Soul

Fresh Sample

You cannot hold back a good laugh any more than you can the tide.
Both are forces of nature.
~William Rotsier

It began as a typical working day. As a registered nurse, I traveled to clients' homes to complete paramedical health assessments for an insurance company.

As I entered this lady's neat, attractive home, I smelled the delicious aroma of pies baking. "Umm, sure smells good in here," I commented.

"I just put a couple of lemon meringue pies in the oven. They're my husband's favorite," my client volunteered.

Returning to the purpose of my visit, we completed the questionnaire quickly. The last section involved collecting a urine sample.

"I collected it earlier and saved it in the refrigerator," she said. "I'll get it for you."

As I emptied the sample into the collection tubes, I noticed the unusual thickness of it. When I tested it with a dip stick, I was shocked at the extremely high protein content.

"Are you sure this is your urine sample?" I questioned. "This almost resembles egg whites."

"Yes, I distinctly remember placing it in the refrigerator in the bottom right-hand corner. Oh! Oh, no!" She wailed. "I've made a terrible mistake. Don't use that. I'll get you a fresh sample."

Not wishing to further embarrass the lady, I asked no more questions. But as I opened the door to leave her home, I heard her removing pies from the oven and the grinding sound of the garbage disposal.

No lemon meringue pie that night!

~Donna McDonnall
Chicken Soup for the Nurse's Soul

I'll Plant Anything

Blessed is he who has learned how to laugh at himself,
for he shall never cease to be entertained.
~John Bowell

A good friend of mine was going away on a long trip during the fall. Miriam thought she had given herself plenty of time to do all the things that are required when one goes out of town.

I called her the day before her departure to wish her bon voyage. She was a wreck. She was completely behind on everything she needed to do. "And to top it all off," she lamented, "I bought some wonderful corms to plant for next spring. I'll never get them into the ground now!"

Well, I'll tell you, I can't bear the thought of an unplanted corm, bulb, seed plug, you name it. I always start too many seeds in March and by June I'm tucking them everywhere I can. I just can't bear the thought of a plant not getting a chance to grow. In other words, she was in luck.

"I'll plant them for you," I said.

"Oh, would you? You would do that?" Miriam was elated. She promised to set them out on the porch for me. I knew her garden well, as we have spent many hours together, toiling in each other's gardens. We quickly brainstormed some nice places for them to go. But then she said, "Oh, just put them wherever you think they'll look nice."

I arrived a couple of days later on a chilly autumn morning and spied a frost-covered paper bag on the back steps. With my trowel and bone meal in hand, I set off in search of just the right place to plant.

The corms were weird-looking—not the usual miniature, root-like bulbs. I hadn't asked what kind they were when Miriam and I had last talked, but the two of us were always trying out new varieties of anything we could get our hands on. Being a consummate experimental gardener, there isn't a lot I won't try to plant and coax through our seemingly endless Minnesota winters. So I shrugged my shoulders and went to work. After a lot of digging, arranging, changing my mind, digging some more and rearranging, I finally stood back from the patch of disturbed earth and nodded to myself in satisfaction. They were all planted in the perfect spot.

When Miriam got back a few months later, she and I went out to dinner to celebrate her return. At the restaurant we laughed about what a wreck she had been when she was trying to get out of town. And then she said, "You know, I still can't believe I forgot to put those corms out! What a ditz brain I am!"

I looked at her quizzically. "What do you mean? Of course you put them out. They were sitting on the porch in a paper bag, right where you said they'd be."

"No," she said, "they're still sitting on the counter where I left them."

Then an expression of dawning realization spread across her face. It held an odd combination of amusement and alarm.

"Valerie, I'm so sorry...."

"What?"

"I'm truly sorry...."

"What?!"

She paused as if to prepare me for her news. Then she slowly said, "That was cat poop."

"What?!"

"Cat poop," she repeated. "I'm afraid I cleaned the litter box out before I left and forgot to put it in the garbage. I guess I must have left it on the back steps. You planted cat poop."

News like this doesn't sink in immediately. It sort of bounces around in your head and all you can hear are the echoes. Cat poop... cat poop....

Miriam looked at my face—and did the best she could to keep from laughing. Tears welled up in her eyes, and she pressed her lips tightly together. I usually have a good sense of humor. But I was too busy replaying the images of me picking these hard little corm-like kernels from a brown paper bag and lovingly planting them in Mother Earth's bosom. I took a long drink of my wine. I wasn't sure I could laugh about this.

Miriam managed to pull herself together. She cleared her throat and, sensing my state of shock, politely asked, "So, where did you plant them?"

"Uh, next to the catnip," I replied. The next thing I knew we both had collapsed into a fit of laughter. Much to my surprise, I was laughing. And it felt good. Very good.

Years have passed since then, and both our gardens and our friendship have continued to grow. That story has grown, too—to become one of our dearest bonds. I guess, true to form, I really will try to plant just about anything.

~Valerie Wilcox
Chicken Soup for the Gardener's Soul

The Night
Al Heel Broke Loose

In a certain northern city, in a certain regional hospital, a story is still whispered about the "Legend of Wanda May." It has grown some over the years, but as one of the few witnesses to the entire chain of events, I will try to stick to the facts.

Wanda, a rookie nurse, was a mighty mite of sorts. Standing four feet, eleven inches, she couldn't have weighed more than ninety pounds, yet every inch of her screamed spitfire! With her green eyes and shiny black hair, Wanda was a looker. Even her cap, which conjured visions of the flying nun, and her oversized scrub suit added to her allure.

Our fifteen-bed ICU ran like organized chaos. With whirring ventilators, beeping monitors, blaring code sirens, ringing phones, glaring lights and chatting nurses, sensory overload was a common problem for our patients. A unique phenomenon known as ICU psychosis afflicts about 10 percent of those treated in this environment. Without warning, a sweet and kindly grandmother could morph into a Linda Blair clone right before your eyes. With proper medication, the condition usually lasts only twenty-four hours. Still, the poor patients are often mortified by their reported behaviors.

On the night in question, the unit was unusually quiet. With only three patients, I stayed at the desk to read the cardiac monitors while Phyllis, a jolly seasoned nurse, looked after two patients. This left

Wanda to care for Alan Heel. Al looked much older than his twenty-seven years; he'd lived a hard life. Kidney disease and his penchant for alcohol proved a difficult combination. His heart strained to pump the extra fluids his body couldn't eliminate. Weekly dialysis is a hard lot in life. Long deserted by family, you could almost understand the root of Al's addiction. He was a frequent patient in our unit, and we all knew it would be a miracle if Al saw thirty. This huge grinning fellow with an unruly shock of black hair loved the attention he received in the unit. And he was never happier than when Wanda was his nurse. He swore she looked exactly like his favorite stripper, and we teased and regaled him with "Hey Big Spender" whenever Wanda was at his bedside. In spite of all of his shortcomings, Al was easy to like.

By midnight on this particular night, the patients were settled and the checks were done. Sitting at the desk, Wanda entertained us with the latest chapter of her ill-fated romantic life. Suddenly, multiple monitor alarms screamed. In the time it took to look up, there was Al, looming over us, huge and naked—except for the monitor leads flapping from his chest. We could have taken his pulse by watching the blood spurting from his thigh where he'd yanked the arterial line. If not for the blood, the absurdity of Al dragging his urine bag might have been comical—but there was nothing funny in his eyes.

Wanda and Phyllis tried to cajole him back to his room. Grabbing the phone, I paged security and then put in a call to his doctor. The next few moments unfolded like a scene from the Keystone Kops!

Al ran, followed by Wanda, Phyllis, two seventy-year-old security guards and several nurses from the step-down unit. He charged from room to room, fleeing a demon only he could see. Patients screamed, guards yelled, staff raced in all directions. The arrival of three police officers and his doctor only added to the chaos. Cornering him in the hallway, they nearly subdued him, but the power of his psychosis proved too great.

When he darted into the four-bed ward in the adjoining step-down unit, panic reigned. The screams of the four elderly female occupants almost drowned out the alarms from their collective heart monitors.

Jumping on top of the nearest bed, Al took a hostage. Now debate often ensues about the weapon Al used. I hear tell now that it was a butcher knife, but to the best of my recollection it was a letter opener he picked up from the patient's tray table. Flipping the poor woman so she was perched on top of his naked body, Al held the letter opener to her neck. The frantic look in his eyes gave us all cause to believe he would use it. Backing off as he demanded, we all tried to think of a way of getting a shot of Valium into him. In this truly desperate, life-threatening situation, the legend of Wanda May was born.

Holding us at arm's length, Wanda stepped forward. Slack-jawed, we watched as she flipped off her cap, undid her braid and fluffed her long, luxurious hair. In a sultry voice, she belted the song, "The minute you walked in the joint...." With her eyes focused on Al's, she pulled her scrub shirt over her head and sent it sailing across the room. His wild eyes softened as she shimmied closer. It was plain to see that the occupant with the "knife" to her throat didn't know which of these evils was greater. In two more seductive moves, Wanda was down to her skivvies. With a crooked finger, she beckoned Al to follow her. As if in a trance, he put down his weapon and rose from the bed. In utter silence, the assembled onlookers parted and Wanda, clad only in bra and panties, walked through the center, with a docile Al directly behind. She continued humming the strains of "Big Spender" all the way back to the unit. Patting Al's bed, she prompted him to lie down. Now I was frightened for Wanda's safety. But instead of venting aggression or male energy, Al began to cry. With his head nestling on her chest, Wanda held him and stroked his hair while the doctor and I started an IV and a flurry of drugs. In moments, an exhausted Al drifted off to sleep. Extricating herself from his grasp, Wanda casually asked, "Could someone get my clothes?"

She may have been small of stature, but Wanda May will forever remain a giant to those who continue to whisper her legend.

~Elizabeth Turner
Chicken Soup for the Nurse's Soul

Woman to Woman

Through the Generations

*I am a reflection of my past generations
and the essence of those following after me.*
~Martha Kinney

Step on a Crack, Bring Your Mother Back

"Step on a crack, break your mother's back," my best friend Franny laughed. She stomped her detested new white bucks on every scar on the cement, giggling. From that call to attention, our walk to school became dangerous. I marveled at her risky rebelliousness as I tiptoed my Mary Janes around the sprung concrete of those New York City sidewalks. I come from a superstitious tribe. A broken Mom was a big threat, something I could never—would never wish on my mother.

These days my mother lives on the Pacific side of the continent in a small group home. Several of the other residents, like my mother, have Alzheimer's disease.

It was no surprise to me when my mother was diagnosed with Alzheimer's. Over a period of years her optimistic eyes began to dim and the mental agility of this eternal student began to disappear. The process was slow and subtle; at first she made jokes about her forgetfulness, but gradually the benign humor vanished, to be replaced by a more severe helplessness. At the memory disorder clinic of a nearby teaching hospital, they described the prognosis; they recommended to me the books I could read that would help. They were kind and caring. The rest of my mother's life, though, seemed a frightening pathway, cracked and distorted by the unpredictable course of a debilitating disease.

"Does she still know you?" This was the first question people asked when I mentioned my mother's disability. Not understanding the slow course of the disease, they always pictured the worst and were surprised and reassured when I told them that my mother did indeed still recognize me. In fact, I told them, her humor surfaced frequently, like when she coyly introduced me as her mother. Her vocabulary was often startlingly original and, with great effort, she still had pockets of usable memory.

A better question emerged: Did I still know her? Who was that woman who looked like my mother but whose eyes could not belie her bewilderment? She was a woman of independence who had lived alone for more than twenty years after my father's death. Unprepared for her sudden widowhood, she learned over the years to manage well on her own, physically, financially and socially. She was determined to survive the poverty of her first generation immigrant upbringing and, finally, in her later years, she came to enjoy a freedom she wasn't raised to expect.

Alzheimer's, a thief in slow motion, stole that freedom and left a woman who could no longer remember her personal history or how many years ago her husband had died. She couldn't recall where her money was or how much it amounted to. Her supposedly golden years were spent living in a house she never called home and enduring a sense of disorientation that she did not understand.

One morning, her arm threaded in mine, we strolled out of her group house for our walk around town. The sidewalk in front of the house was slowly giving way to a mighty cedar tree that dwarfed the Victorian structure.

Suddenly, my boot wedged in a deep crevice in the walkway, and I was pitched forward. My mother reacted instantly, making her arm rigid and yanking me upright. I regained my composure and smiled at her gratefully.

"Are you okay?" she asked with concern. I looked at her, and the thrill of recognition gave me goose bumps. My old Mom, the Mom that I had always known, was smiling at me, her eyes clear, bright with the light of purpose, not a trace of confusion evident.

For a brief moment, my mind flashed back to another time, many, many years ago, when I had seen my mother smile at me in just that way. It was a rainy winter's day in Queens, New York. The weather had been stormy all week and our '54 Plymouth didn't like the rain any more than we did. It stalled just after we picked up my father's shirts at the cleaners. As we sat together in the car, patiently awaiting the tow truck, my mother took my rain boots off and tickled my feet under her coat. We laughed and talked as a car pulled up and parked behind us on the downward incline of a slight hill. A woman in a red kerchief and dark coat sprinted to a shop across the street. Something in the rearview mirror caught my mother's attention. In a flash, she thrust open the car door and swooped me out into the street as the car behind us rolled from its parking spot and slammed our Plymouth into the car parked in front. But we were safe. I huddled against her in the rain, peering up with surprise. She hugged me closer and smiled with relief.

"Are you okay?"

She needn't have asked. Of course I was. I was in my mother's arms.

Those same arms now wrapped around me after my stumble on the sidewalk, and that same smile reassured me.

"I love you so much," she said as she kissed me. "I don't want anything to happen to you." I had heard her say this many times in my life but not recently. I felt overjoyed to have her back.

We continued on down the street where we had walked several times a week since I moved her closer to me. "I haven't been on this street in years," she announced. As she turned to me for confirmation, something she does often given the erratic universe of her mind, I saw that my real mother had slipped away again.

Nothing in my life could have prepared me for the complicated task of caring for a parent with Alzheimer's. Our tender relationship has become an act of balancing familiarity with strangeness. It is one thing to grieve for a parent gone; it is quite another to have to learn to love one you still have but no longer know.

Even though I see my mother often, I miss her very much. I

keep looking forward to the next time I might stumble across her endearing old self, feel her love wrap around me and, if only for a moment, keep me shielded from the pain of losing her.

~Sandra Rockman
Chicken Soup for the Mother's Soul 2

20

The Blessing of Old Age

Happiness is an attitude.
We either make ourselves miserable, or happy and strong.
The amount of work is the same.
~Francesca Reigler

My coworkers and I had lunch together every day. As with any group of women, our conversation ranged from our families and work to our female problems. One day, the conversation centered on our litany of complaints over getting older.

One coworker described her hot flashes in detail, how in the middle of the night she got out of bed, got naked and lay on the cool tile floor in her bathroom to calm her night sweats. Another described dressing and undressing constantly depending on her body temperature. One woman commented that between her mood swings and arthritis, her family compared her to Dr. Jekyll and Mr. Hyde, never knowing what personality was going to show up next. They all bemoaned the fact that their behinds had spread and that they seemed to work harder to try to maintain a decent weight. Then there was the existential question: "My life is half over and what have I done with it?"

Throughout this entire conversation, I remained silent, listening to their complaints. Finally, one woman turned to me. "You're going to be fifty this year. You must have some complaints."

I smiled and sipped my tea. "Well, I guess I look at age differently.

Sure, I wish I were twenty pounds lighter, and I have hot flashes and bursitis in my shoulder, but I can live with those things. But you know what? I can't wait to turn fifty. I'm finally starting my writing career and I feel great. I'm looking forward to getting my AARP card and never paying full price for anything anymore."

Everyone laughed, but I could tell by their curious looks that they thought I was just a little strange.

"My mother died of cancer when she was forty-eight years old. She never got to experience what I'm experiencing now," I said. My coworkers suddenly became quiet. "So I welcome old age with all its aches and pains. Old age is a blessing, and that's just how I'm going to treat it."

"You know, I never thought of it that way," one woman said. "I guess you're right."

Suddenly, the conversation changed from the aches and pains of old age to older persons they knew who were still active, and how they hoped to be like them. Old age, they agreed, might have its aches and pains, but it was indeed a blessing. A blessing to be embraced with an open heart and mind.

~Sharon M. Stanford
Chicken Soup to Inspire a Woman's Soul

21

The Tablecloth

It takes a long time to grow an old friend.
~John Leonard

Last year, my mother, Rose, lost her best friend of fifty years, Rosa, to cancer. Over a lifetime, Mom and Rosa forged a relationship that transcended the two of them, tightly intertwining their families as well. The two women knew and understood each other thoroughly and plainly, and deeply valued each other's company and wisdom.

Their friendship began when they were young brides, inviting each other to barbecues and cocktail parties where they tried out and polished their cooking skills. A few years later, each became pregnant, beginning parallel journeys of motherhood. As the years passed, together they experienced the normal ups and downs of raising a family, providing one another with daily comfort, encouragement and companionship.

When Rosa's cancer was diagnosed, my mother was her greatest cheerleader. Galvanized by fear and a loss of control, Mom organized meals, shuttled Rosa to doctor appointments, ministered to Rosa's husband and grown children, and when possible, translated medical lingo to a bewildered family. My mother, a quintessential helper, gave Rosa and her loved ones much-needed support, gratified to be the scaffolding on which her fragile friend leaned.

Rosa's prognosis was poor from the start, and within a year, she died. As arrangements for the funeral were made, Mom, herself grief-stricken, played a critical role stabilizing Rosa's family and assisting with important decisions. The fact that she was needed was, of course, good therapy as she struggled through her own emotions.

Shortly after Rosa passed away, her bereaved husband, Jean, called my mother on behalf of their daughter, Marsha, who lived out of town. "Rose," he said, "when Marsha was here for the funeral she turned the house upside down looking for a tablecloth she said Rosa had been working on, embroidery or something. I have no idea where it is, and Marsha is devastated about it. I think Rosa was working on it for her. Do you have any idea where she might have put it?"

The next day, my mother, her heart heavy with loss, pulled up in front of her friend's house. Walking into the dining room, fifty years of knowing Rosa's habits her guide, she opened the bottom drawer of the china cabinet, revealing the tablecloth and napkins Marsha was searching for. Unfolding the embroidered cloth, she said to Jean, "I remember Rosa telling me about this cloth before she became sick. She was working on it for Marsha, but it looks like she finished only half of it before she had to give it up. Do you mind if I finish it?"

My mother carried the cloth home and lovingly studied her friend's handiwork. With tears in her eyes but with a sense of renewal, she threaded the embroidery needle tucked into the fabric and began to sew. For days, she embroidered, each stitch fortifying and healing her.

The tablecloth finished and ironed, Mom draped it over her lap, examining the commingling of her stitches with Rosa's, contemplating the weight of their joint effort and thinking how true it is that the whole is much more than the sum of its parts. With great care, she swaddled the cloth in tissue, placed it in a box and mailed it to the daughter of her best friend.

~Bohne G. Silber
Chicken Soup for the Girlfriend's Soul

The Mirror Has Three Faces

And thou shalt in thy daughter see,
This picture, once, resembled thee.
~Ambrose Philips

I am fifty-one years old. My mother was fifty-one when she died. I remember that last day of her life only too clearly. It was a rainy Monday, and my mother could not breathe.

"It's fluid," the doctor said. "We'll tap her lungs." They sat my mother up in the hospital bed and plunged the long needle through her back into her lungs. Again and again they tried, but no fluid came. And no relief.

"It's not fluid," the doctor said. "It's all tumor. We can't help her breathe."

I remember my mother's desperate words. "I can't... breathe. Turn up the oxygen... please." But turning up the oxygen didn't help. Her lungs, bursting with cancer, fought to make room for the air. My mother whispered her final words to me, "I want the quickest way."

My mother should have grown old. Her dark hair, peppered with gray, should have become snowy white. The fine lines, etched in her face from her smiles, should have become soft wrinkles. Her quick step should have given way to a slower, more seasoned gait.

My mother should have watched her five grandchildren grow

up. She should have had the chance to enfold them in her very special brand of love and to impart to them her considerable wisdom. She should have been arm in arm with my father—she was the only girl he ever loved—sojourning into their shared golden years. She didn't. She wasn't. She never had the chance. She was fifty-one, and she died.

I was twenty-seven when my mother died. Over the years, not a day went by when I didn't think of something I wanted to tell her, to ask her or to show her. I railed bitterly against the injustice of it. It wasn't fair that my mother died at fifty-one.

Now I am fifty-one. I look into the mirror and it strikes me: I have slowly but surely been transformed. There she is with that gray peppered hair, those dark intense eyes, that expression on my face. When I hear my voice, it is her voice. I have become my mother.

I am entering a new and strange stage of my life. I have always looked ahead to see my mother. Ever so briefly, I stood next to her. Now I'm beginning to be older than my mother. The direction in which I gaze to see her will change. Soon I will look back at my mother.

Gradually my mother will become young in comparison with me. I will grow old instead of her—acquire the white hair she should have had but never did. I will develop that seasoned gait she never experienced, see those soft facial wrinkles she never had, and so it will continue on and on until one day when I'm seventy-five, as she would have been today. On that day, the reversal of our roles complete, I will turn around to look at her, but see instead my own daughter, at fifty-one—my mother.

~Kristina Cliff-Evans
Chicken Soup for the Golden Soul

Emma's Bouquets

It was a hot June day when my mother and I crossed the Texas border and made our way to Minden, west of Shreveport, Louisiana. Although it wasn't far to the old George family farm, where my great-grandparents had homesteaded 100 years earlier, I had never been there before.

As we drew closer to the family homestead, through softly rolling hills of longleaf pine, sweet gum and red oak, I thought about what connects us with earlier generations of our family. Is it just a matter of eye color, height or blood type? Or are there other ties that bind us? If my great-grandmother Emma could find her way into the present, would she discover something familiar in my generation?

When my mom and I turned into the George property, we saw before us a real Southern farmhouse — mostly porch with a house attached. Although it was just a simple farmhouse, its front windows were graced with ornately carved dental moldings, and the steps from the porch — flanked by large brick pillars with granite plinths — were a palatial ten feet wide. The house bore a startling resemblance to the houses my brother and sister and I owned, even though none of us had ever seen this place. When I'd bought my old farmhouse in North Carolina, for example, the first thing I'd done was to add a replica of this porch. Similarly, my brother's and sister's Louisiana homes, although newly designed by architects, bore an uncanny resemblance to the old George homestead.

As my mother and I strolled through the garden, where roses, day lilies, irises, vitex and phlox still bloomed, my mother remarked, "Your great-grandmother Emma loved flowers." Wanting to keep a part of this, my heritage, I knelt down and dug out one of the iris pips.

Because I also wanted to preserve something from the inside of the house, before it crumbled and was lost to time, we gingerly explored the interior, noting the twenty-inch-wide virgin pine boards, the hand-hewn beams and the handmade clay bricks, each marked with a G. Then, in the bedroom, I discovered Emma's 1890s wallpaper—a floral motif, naturally, with a repeating pattern of large bouquets of ivory and pink roses. It was peeling off the pine boards, but still lovely after all this time, just like my great-grandmother's garden. I knew this was the memento I wanted to take with me. With the tiny penknife on my key ring, I carved off two square-foot pieces, one for me and one for my younger sister, Cindy.

Before we headed for home, Mom and I stood on that familiar front porch for a moment of silent leave-taking.

At that instant, I felt very connected to my ancestors, as though there were invisible wires running between us, anchoring each successive generation to the earlier ones. However, on the drive home, I began to wonder if I weren't making too much of this family ties thing. Perhaps a penchant for wide porches was just a coincidence.

The next day, eager to share the story of this trip with Cindy, I dropped by her house. I found her in the kitchen, happily perusing the materials she had bought on a recent trip to England in order to redecorate her home. We sat at the table together, and I told her about our great-grandparents' farmhouse with its verandah, floor-to-ceiling windows and high ceilings that had somehow found their way into the design of the homes of the Georges' great-grandchildren. We laughed about my muddying my dress in order to dig out a flower pip, and then I produced the little square of wallpaper I'd brought for her as a keepsake.

She appeared stunned, sitting stone-still and dead-quiet. I thought I had, in my big-sister way, offended her with my story. Then she reached into the box of her renovation materials and pulled out the rolls of newly purchased wallpaper from England. The design was exactly the same—the ivory-pink sprays and bouquets of roses were Emma's.

Emma's bouquets had found their way into the present.

~Pamela George
A Second Chicken Soup for the Woman's Soul

Woman to Woman

Inner Strength and Courage

*Wisdom is meaningless until
our own experience has given it meaning.*
~Bergen Evans

24

Starting Over

Courage is the power to let go of the familiar.
~Raymond Lindquist

y husband of twenty-five years had died only three weeks before, and I was alone—running a business and worried about keeping house and home together. Everyone remarked how well I was doing. I looked composed on the surface and was comforted by the convincing role I was playing. But frightening questions arose when I didn't expect them. Could the business support my daughter Lexi and me without Paul helping us run it? Where would we move if I had to sell our house? Most frightening of all, I was terrified that if I surrendered to my grief, let myself really feel it, I would be sucked downward into a dark, bottomless spiral from which I would never return to sanity. I knew I had to do something.

Several years earlier, Paul and I had been very impressed by a man named Tim Piering. He helped people work through their deepest fears by leading them through the very things they were most afraid of. I decided to make an appointment with him.

The following Saturday, I drove to Tim's office in Sierra Madre, located in the foothills of the San Gabriel Mountains in Southern California. Tim, a tall ex-Marine with a big heart, asked me questions and listened to me for a while, then asked if Paul would want me to grieve for him. I thought about it.

"No, I can't imagine that he would. In fact, I think he'd strongly object."

"I'm sure he'd object, and I really think I can help, Diana. I think we can process some of the grief you're feeling, and lessen it. Would you like to try?"

"Y-yes," I managed to say. It was as if I wanted to hold onto my hidden grief out of loyalty to Paul, although I knew he'd want me to do everything I could to move ahead.

"Notice the thoughts going on in your head," Tim said. "All your fears, your considerations, sound like radio voices, don't they? Of all these thoughts, fear is the most debilitating. Not only does it sap your energy, but it also will cost you many great opportunities. Just think of how many times you have held back from doing something because of fear. If you are willing, Diana, I'm going to give you a quick course in stretching your ability to do anything you want to do. Basically, what will happen is you will have a completely new image of yourself, and you will see how you can take any action—any action you want—regardless of what your mind is saying. Your mind can be yakking away, even screaming, and you can go ahead and do things in spite of the racket going on in your mind."

Tim drove me in his truck high into the nearby mountains. He pulled onto a shoulder and parked. Carrying ropes and other equipment from the back of his sports utility vehicle, he led me out onto a bridge that spanned a dry wash several hundred feet below. I watched as Tim attached a pulley to the bridge railing and to his body and threaded the pulleys with ropes. Suddenly, he climbed over the railing and lowered himself slowly to the bottom of the canyon. Climbing back up the hill, he called, "Want to try it yourself?"

"Not on your life!"

Tim went over the side once again, showing me how he could maneuver up and down with the pulley, and how a safety rope was in place just in case. It did seem very safe, and I began to feel I could do it, and said I might try it someday.

With that small crack showing in my armor of fear, Tim wasted no time strapping the gear on me and attaching the rope to my rappelling ring. He showed me how to gradually roll the pulley and come to a complete stop during the descent. He attached the safety rope to himself.

"Okay, now just step over the railing."

"Ha! Easy for you to say!"

"It's a metaphor, Diana, for how willing you are to really 'go for the gold' in your life."

I've never, ever felt more terrified. Since childhood I've been afraid of heights and had recurring nightmares of teetering on a cliff or window ledge. I trembled at the mere thought of standing on the outside of the railing. Very, very slowly I eased one leg over the railing, saying, "Oh, my God, I am so scared!"

Tim held both of my hands firmly on the railing as I lifted the other leg over, leaning as far toward him as I could for protection. My heart was pounding and I began to whimper.

"Let's just forget the whole thing!"

"It's your decision, Diana. You don't have to do it."

No one was making me do this, I realized. I'd come to Tim for help. I had a hunch that if I could only do this, it would make all the difference. Again, I resolved to try.

"Okay, I'm going to do it. I'm committed."

"Let go with one hand and hold the rope tightly so you won't start moving until you're ready."

I was bleating like a terrified sheep, I was so frightened. But I did what Tim said—I let go of the railing with one hand. Then came the crucial moment. I released the other hand—and there I was, swinging in small arcs over the canyon.

So far, so good.

"Now—very slowly—inch your way down a foot or two."

I did. At that moment, my fear was transformed to excitement. It was easy for me to operate the pulley. I took a long time lowering myself to the bottom, relishing the view and my victory over the terrified voice in my head. Tim ran down to meet me.

"Look what you did, Diana! You did it!"

And so I had. Li'l old me, exactly like a U.S. Marine! Wow! If I could do that, I could do anything! I thought to myself. I felt elated and more powerful than I ever had before.

Then Tim took me to a firing range and had me fire an automatic revolver repeatedly, another thing I would never have dreamed of doing. I realize now that Tim wanted me to feel a different kind of fear than what a woman—suddenly alone—would normally feel. Survival in a physical sense—not an emotional one. I could feel my life beginning again.

"Diana, you've stretched your reality of what you thought you could do. This is a benchmark that will allow you to rise to new levels of action in spite of fear. Whenever you feel confronted by an action you need to take, you can think back to this experience, and whatever challenges you face will seem easy in comparison. This one short event—committing to the action of going off the bridge—will propel you years ahead in how you operate in scary situations. And it will stretch your limits for all the things that frighten you. Regardless of your thoughts, you can do almost anything just because you commit to doing it. You've opened the door to the possibility of achieving all your dreams, Diana.

"In the beginning, you may spend most of your time fighting the negative comments of the radio voices that try to justify all the reasons why you shouldn't do something. But, as you remember what you accomplished here today, Diana, keep this thought in mind: The world owes you nothing. You've landed on the playing field of life. The only question is: will you play?"

~Diana von Welanetz Wentworth
Chicken Soup to Inspire the Body and Soul

25

Dancing for Fireflies

Other things may change us, but we start and end with the family.
~Anthony Brandt

On a Saturday morning a few years back, I made a difficult and irreversible decision. My daughter was at the piano, galloping through *Unchained Melody*. My son was polishing the hallway mirrors, eager to earn a few extra dollars for a new CD. I couldn't decide if it was the warm mug of coffee cupped in my hands—brewed just right for a change—or the sense of harmony that seemed out of character in a house that had become a war zone as of late, but I realized how crucial it is that a home be a peaceful place away from the turmoil of work and school. And, in those moments, a startling thought welled up in me. I suddenly realized that little by little, I was jeopardizing the greatest source of safety my children can possess: the home that my husband and I have provided for them.

A safe home has little to do with physical elements, even though we judge other people's homes by the craftsmanship of the woodwork or the quality of the drapes. I'm referring to the "atmosphere" of a home—or maybe "soul" is the definitive word. I recall one weekend years ago, visiting a college friend's elaborate home. I was so impressed that each bedroom had its own bathroom with the thickest, most luxurious towels. Yet that detail seemed marred by the chilling silence that existed between her parents—a silence so loud that I still recall it vividly. I also remember a rather ramshackle house on the outskirts of my hometown. The lady who lived there was a seamstress, a kind woman who listened with eyes that smiled through peculiar blue-rimmed glasses. Whenever my mother took me for a fitting, I was never quite ready to leave. One evening when I went to pick up a dress, she and her husband, Eddie, with the oil-field grime scrubbed from his skin, sat at the table with their kids. They were eating peach cobbler, laughing loudly and playing Yahtzee, and on that evening, their home, with its worn furniture and framed paint-by-number artwork, was clearly one of the finest.

Uncontrollable hardships may plague a home's well-being: the loss of a job, a serious illness or even death. But it's the circumstances many of us encounter on a day-to-day basis that often wear us down and more often contribute to the breakup of a home. I know many couples just like my husband and myself. Once upon a time each other's company charmed us. Our infatuation with each other seemed to cast a rosy glow over the fact that we could barely make ends meet as we struggled to balance part-time jobs with our college classes. Our furniture was the cast-offs our relatives were glad to unload, we guarded the thermostat with a frugal eye, and tomato soup was a common meal staple. Yet the two of us created a mansion with our passion. We graduated, found our niche in the working world, bought our first house, and when our children came along, we were even more enchanted with the cozy feeling their wide-eyed wonder contributed to our home. Long walks with the stroller, Dr. Seuss, dancing for fireflies in the warm twilight—we were happy.

But somehow twenty years passed and neither my husband nor I could account for the past five. Our jobs demanded more of our time, and our passion for each other slipped away so gradually I scarcely noticed. Our children grew older and fought more so we bought a house twice as big where we were soon spending our time in four remote corners: my husband with his work or evening TV, I with my nose in a pile of bills, my daughter's ear glued to the tele-phone, and my son, depending on his moods, lost in the world of alternative music or ESPN. When my husband and I did talk, it was to argue about how to discipline adolescent angst, or whose turn it was to take out the garbage. What happened to the long walks, "Sam I Am" and the fireflies?

On that Saturday morning months ago, I faced a reality I had been denying. Something I never imagined could happen to me, had happened. I grew dependent on the attention of another man. Despite his graying hair, he's uncannily like the strong-willed but sensitive guy who charmed me almost two decades ago. Our friendship sparkled because we'd never raised headstrong children, never lived together during hay-fever season, and never woken up to each other's foul breath or puffy eyes. We had never experienced any of the tribulations, minor or major, which test and shape a relationship. In the months that followed, visits with him had grown more intense and drew me farther away from my husband, the other anchor in our children's home. In fact, I had actually begun to imagine life without the man I had promised to love until my last breath.

And so, in one of the saddest and most awkward moments of my life, I told my friend that I could no longer see him. I ended a friendship with a person who had begun to matter very much to me. As I struggled to abandon my feelings for him and embrace the logic of closing the door, the days which followed were filled with a frightening revelation: somehow, unthinkingly, when half of marriages end in divorce, I had threatened our home with the most common reason: a lack of commitment. I had pursued a selfish desire to the point that I could no longer distinguish between right and wrong. I had been entrusted with a loyal husband and two remarkable children, yet I risked their well-being with every moment I spent in this other person's company.

After my decision, there was a wave of emptiness that continually washed through me as I moved through each day. I felt it when I lay awake next to my husband who snored peacefully at three in the morning. It came again at work when my mind drifted away from the pile of paperwork in front of me or the discussion at a meeting. It welled up once more as I sat on the front porch with the evening paper, and my two kids fought over the basketball in the driveway.

Gradually, though, that feeling has been replaced with a sense of relief that, despite my temporary insanity, my family is safe. But a thousand "I'm sorries" will never take away the sting of remorse I feel nearly every time I look in my husband's eyes and they smile back at me. While the passion we first had doesn't always seem as strong, passion is meaningless compared with the qualities he possesses. I hadn't a clue how much I would come to value his integrity, his work ethic or his devotion to our children. It wasn't until I was confronted with the fear of losing the world that he and I had created together, that I recognized the pricelessness of his friendship.

So tonight, on an unusually warm evening for this time of year, my husband has agreed to join me for a walk. As I study the sky from the window by my desk, I see that there must be a thousand stars tonight, all sparkling like fireflies.

~Sarah Benson
Chicken Soup for Every Mom's Soul

26

Wild Waters Run Deep

If we wait for our hands to stop shaking, we will never open the door.
~Naomi Newman

No doubt about it, a fortieth birthday requires a spectacular celebration. So I did what I thought a self-respecting, bold woman who has learned that she is responsible for her happiness might do—I decided to make my own party and take it with me! That my celebration took place in a foreign country, where I was alone, surrounded by a group of strangers and involved a near-death experience that coincided with my birthday was grist for the mill.

I decided to go white-water rafting because it was something new and wild and adventurous that would push the fear envelope. As Eleanor Roosevelt said, "You must do the thing you think you cannot do." White-water rafting through class IV and class V rapids down the Rio Pacuare in the Costa Rican rain forest seemed like just the ticket! So, I packed my Spanish tape, water bottle, bathing suit, sandals and sunscreen, and set off for my "Fortieth Birthday White-Water Rafting Adventure of a Lifetime." Little did I know, wild waters run deep.

I should have taken it as a premonition when our bus made a pit stop along the road to the river where a vendor was selling "I survived Rio Pacuare" T-shirts. I bought one and put it on; people on the bus with me all laughed! Maybe I should have thought better of getting in a raft with a group of total strangers, most who had never rafted before, and going down a river with such potential danger. And, it probably is not the best thing to be with guides who speak limited English and give only cursory lessons in rafting, which mostly included telling us to hold on, a lot. And, maybe there is something to the proliferative liability laws that we have in the United States, at least as far as the safety protection they may offer toward the assumption of risk.

Well, you probably guessed it. Not too long into the experience, I was knocked out of the raft, went over a small waterfall into a whirlpool (they call it a "hydraulic"; I call it "hell") and got sucked to the bottom of the river in a swirling confusion of water. And that was just the beginning of the ride. Fortunately, I did have on a helmet and life jacket. I can't imagine what I would have done without them. Nevertheless, I did get quite an exfoliation from the numerous rocks I hit, not to mention all the water I swallowed.

While I was busy getting more than I bargained for, I had an epiphany about life. While being tossed about by those wonderful, wild waters and flopping in and out of submersion like a rag doll, my mind took me to another place. Somehow, I got my feet pointed downstream as you're supposed to. And, I did my best to keep my head above water as much as possible, which, actually, was nearly impossible. It was horrible trying to breathe and not being able to get enough air. But, I became incredibly calm, despite the sheer terror of the situation and the possibility that I might die.

I thought, Oh wow. I fell into the river in the middle of a rapid. Boy, this really hurts my lungs to try to breathe. Hmmm. Wow. Hey, I might die! I actually felt pretty neutral about the whole thing, living or dying, that is, and I had a strange sort of peacefulness and the ability to watch myself almost from the outside. Maybe all those Buddhist meditation exercises and books about "mindfulness" had paid off!

They tell me that the primary reason I survived that day is precisely because I did not fight the river, because I did not try to swim against the almighty power of rushing water, because I did, in a sense, surrender to the experience. I let the river take me where it would. I actually went through three whirlpools, and each time it got easier.

The drama that day was high magnitude. All the other rafters pulled over to the shore. People were crying and praying and most just looked on with terror at what was unfolding. There were several ropes across the river and three experienced kayakers went in for my rescue. It was quite a scene.

Later, the guides talked about how amazingly polite I was during my rescue. I don't remember that at all. Inside, I am pretty sure I felt like grabbing some guy by the shirt and growling, "Get me out of here, now!" But, in reality, they say that when a kayak came toward me, I simply held out my hand and arm and meekly said, "Could you please help me?" Please? I said that? I learned that often a rescuer is nearly drowned by someone who desperately wants out of the river.

I was dragged to shore and given medical attention and lots of people cheered and some pretty cute Costa Rican guys were all giving me high-fives. I enjoyed the moment and the attention I was getting, until they told me I had to get back in the raft and continue down the river. I really did not want to do that at all, but I found out I had no choice. Also, I could tell everyone's morale seemed to be hanging on my getting back in that raft and going on.

Not feeling very brave, I did go on. I got through the whole course of the river and lived to tell about it. I do have to admit to hunkering down in the middle of the raft a few times when I was supposed to be paddling, but I was scared, and that was the best I could do.

One thing I learned that day is that your best is all you can do and that is exactly what you should do—and your best is very often good enough. Sometimes you fall out of the raft and have to get back in and continue on down the river. And sometimes the best way to get through a difficulty is to just let it be! Don't fight it. Let it be difficult. Know that that is what is happening and that your reaction to it, is what it is. Surrender doesn't mean doing nothing, being passive. Or being perfect. On the contrary, it is a very active thing to let yourself have the experience and not try to control it.

Certainly, I will always remember how I survived that day and how I handled the challenge—who could forget? Even more important, I will carry with me always and be grateful for the lessons I learned from those "wild waters" about how to live my life.

~Benita Tobin
Chicken Soup to Inspire a Woman's Soul

You Can Do Anything!

The only disability in life is a bad attitude.
~Scott Hamilton

I was a twenty-year-old nursing student in 1968, preparing for a rotation through the pediatric unit. Compared to cardiac units or the operating room, how hard would this be? After all, I'd always cared for and played with children. This rotation would be a snap. I'd breeze right through it and be one step closer to graduation.

Chris was an eight-year-old bundle of energy who excelled in every sport he played. Disobeying his parents' instructions, he explored a neighbor's construction site, climbed a ladder and fell. His broken arm was casted too tightly, leading to infection, sepsis and gangrene. Sadly, his condition required amputation.

I was assigned as his postoperative nurse.

The first few days passed quickly. I provided Chris's physical care with forced cheerfulness. His parents stayed with him around the clock.

As his need for medication decreased, his level of awareness increased, as did his moodiness. When I saw how alert he seemed as he watched me bring in supplies for a sponge bath, I offered him the washcloth and suggested he take over. He washed his face and neck, then quit. I finished.

The next day, I announced he'd be in charge of his whole bath.

He balked. I insisted. He was more than halfway through when he slumped down and said, "I'm too tired."

"You won't be in the hospital much longer," I urged gently. "You need to learn to take care of yourself."

"Well, I can't," he scowled. "How can I do anything with just one hand?"

Putting on my brightest face, I groped for a silver lining. Finally I said, "Sure you can do it, Chris. At least you have your right hand."

He turned his face away and muttered, "I'm left-handed. At least I used to be." He glared at me. "Now what?"

Suddenly, I didn't feel so snappy. I felt phony and insincere, and not very helpful. How could I have taken right-handedness for granted? It seemed he and I both had a lot to learn.

The next morning, I greeted Chris with a big smile and a rubber band. He looked at me suspiciously. Wrapping the rubber band loosely around my wrist, I said, "You're left-handed and I'm right-handed. I am going to put my right hand behind my back and keep it there by winding the rubber band around my uniform buttons. Every time I ask you to do something with your right hand, I will do it first, with my left hand. And I promise not to practice before I see you. What should we try first?"

"I just woke up," he grumbled. "I need to brush my teeth."

I managed to screw the top off the toothpaste, then placed his toothbrush on the overbed table. Awkwardly, I tried to squirt toothpaste onto the wobbly toothbrush. The harder I struggled, the more interested he became. After almost ten minutes, and a lot of wasted toothpaste, I succeeded.

"I can do it faster than that!" Chris declared. And when he did, his triumphant grin was just as real as mine.

The next two weeks passed quickly. We tackled his daily activities with enthusiasm and a competitive spirit. We buttoned his shirts, buttered his bread and never really mastered tying his shoes. Despite our age difference, we were playing a game as equal competitors.

By the time my rotation ended, he was almost ready for discharge, and ready to face the world with more confidence. We hugged each other goodbye with sincere friendship and tears.

More than thirty years have passed since our time together. I've encountered some ups and downs in my life, but I've never let a physical challenge pass without thinking of Chris and wondering how he would cope. Sometimes I put a hand behind my back, hook my thumb in my belt and give it a try.

And anytime I feel sorry for myself, for some petty grievance or another, I take myself into the bathroom and try once again to brush my teeth with my left hand.

~Susan M. Goldberg
Chicken Soup for the Nurse's Soul

28

Beauty Contest

Beauty is not in the face; beauty is a light in the heart.
~Kahlil Gibran

A successful beauty product company asked the people in a large city to send brief letters about the most beautiful women they knew, along with the women's pictures. Within a few weeks, thousands of letters were delivered to the company.

One letter in particular caught the attention of the employees, and soon it was handed to the company president. The letter was written by a young boy, who wrote he was from a broken home, living in a run-down neighborhood. With spelling corrections, an excerpt from his letter read:

> *A beautiful woman lives down the street from me. I visit her every day. She makes me feel like the most important kid in the world. We play checkers and she listens to my problems. She understands me and when I leave, she always yells out the door that she's proud of me.*

The boy ended his letter by saying, *"This picture shows you that she is the most beautiful woman. I hope I have a wife as pretty as her."*

Intrigued by the letter, the president asked to see this woman's picture. His secretary handed him a photograph of a smiling, toothless woman, well-advanced in years, sitting in a wheelchair. Sparse gray hair was pulled back in a bun and wrinkles that formed deep furrows on her face were somehow diminished by the twinkle in her eyes.

"We can't use this woman," explained the president, smiling. "She would show the world that our products aren't necessary to be beautiful."

~Carla Muir
A Second Chicken Soup for the Woman's Soul

Woman to Woman

It's All a Matter of Perspective

Nobody trips over mountains.
It is the small pebble that causes you to stumble.
Pass all the pebbles in your path and you will find
you have crossed the mountain.
~Source Unknown

29

Body Work

If you don't like something change it;
if you can't change it, change the way you think about it.
~Mary Engelbreit

I remember the moment when it first happened, the first time I found myself dissatisfied with my body. I was fourteen, lying on my back. I noticed with displeasure that my stomach did not curve inward the way my friend Lisa's did.

Since then I have been on a roller coaster ride. I have been alternately pleased by and disgusted with my body. I have received some positive comments—but also many negative ones—about my physique. One time while out jogging, I heard a man yell out to me, "Keep it up! You need to do a lot of running!" Even my family has gotten into the act, telling me when I am "plump" or advising me when my face has gotten "full."

I have had ambivalent feelings about my body most of my life. Pretty women—reed thin women—reap the rewards in our society, whether it's men, attention or jobs. If a woman is not attractive—and slender—she is ignored. So, like most women, I have wanted to be slim. But I have never gone on a strict diet or embarked on a rigorous exercise program. Clearly, part of me desires to have the perfect body while another part wishes it weren't so important.

A couple of years ago, I started volunteering for the Meals on Wheels chapter in my community. The people I brought meals to certainly weren't obsessing over their appearance and their weight. They had more important things to think about, such as long-term illnesses and perilous financial situations. I realized then that striving for the perfect body is a superficial pursuit, to say the least.

I realized something further. There is only so much I can do to alter my shape. I can exercise regularly and eat healthfully, but I will never measure up to the impossible ideal our society has set. Sure, there's starvation and plastic surgery, but I prefer not to resort to such extreme and potentially dangerous methods.

On the other hand, there is a lot I can do about my feelings of compassion for those less fortunate, my understanding of cultures different from my own and my actions on behalf of people not as healthy and fit as I am. I have decided to focus on these pursuits rather than the futile quest for a better body.

After all, I would rather be admired for the breadth of my kindness than the length of my legs, the size of my heart than the fullness of my breasts, and the shape of my thoughts rather than the proportions of my body. It's taken me twenty-seven years, but I've learned to love my body—after all, it's where I live.

~Carol Ayer
Chicken Soup to Inspire a Woman's Soul

Gifts

The greatest discovery of my generation is that
a human being can alter his life by altering his attitudes.
~William James

I worked closely with Mother Teresa for over thirty years. One day, after my conversation had been filled with a litany of problems, some seemingly insoluble, Mother Teresa remarked, "Everything is a problem. Isn't there another word?"

I confessed that I knew no other word that carried the same weight.

"Why not use the word 'gift'?" she suggested.

With that I began a shift in vocabulary.

One of the first times that this new vocabulary came into use was on our return to New York City from a conference in Vancouver. She had tried without success to be excused from the conference and was extremely anxious to have time with the sisters in New York.

I was dismayed to learn that the trip had to be broken en route with a long delay. I was about to explain the "problem" when I caught myself and said, "Mother, I have to tell you about a gift. We have to wait four hours here, and you won't arrive at the convent until very late."

Mother Teresa agreed that it was indeed a great "gift." She settled down in the airport to read and ponder a favorite book of meditations.

From that time on, items that presented disappointments or difficulties would be introduced with, "We have a small gift here," or "Today we have an especially big gift." Now there were smiles at situations that earlier had been described by the dour word "problem."

~Eileen Egan
Chicken Soup for the Traveler's Soul

31

Happy Birthday

I've really been good the past four days: low-fat cottage cheese, tuna salad with lemon, broiled chicken with broccoli (no butter), grapefruit for breakfast.... Oh boy, I can hardly wait to step on the scale today. Slide out of bed slowly, stretch, savor the anticipated report from the scale. Slip off my robe, step lightly on the scale, look down with fragile confidence. I wonder how many pounds I've lost. Two, three, four maybe? Relishing the anticipated news, I let my eyes slip down to the mechanical device beneath my feet.... Disbelief! Confidence destroyed! Not only did I not lose four pounds, I gained one! I've been tricked, fooled, betrayed. The scale says I've been bad; the scale says I'm fat. Four minutes ago I didn't think so, but now I do. I'm fat. I'm bad. Devastated by the condemnation from the scale, I skulk back to bed wearing my robe like a shroud.

I am accustomed to stepping on the scale in the morning and to having the weight report determine what kind of a mood I will be in for that day. But today I am thirty-four, and I've been dieting in preparation for my birthday. I wanted to feel good today, not old and... But the scale has passed judgment on me: I'm fat. I'm bad. Sullenly I trudge back to bed where I feel, not think, the memories.

I remember.

I am four. My cousins romp circles around me, their loud obnoxious shrieks assaulting my ears. I suppose my quiet granddaddy loves them, too (though I don't know why), but I also know he loves me best. I don't know how I know this, but I do. Though he can hear them—they all scream so loud—and he can hardly hear me at all. My family doesn't talk loudly. We talk quietly in my house, and I talk quietest of all. But Grandpa and I don't talk much; we don't need to. Grandpa, I want to pick pink rhubarb I think, looking up at him. "Shall we go pick some rhubarb, Wee Ann?" he says quietly, taking my small, pudgy hand in his coarse, big one. Grandpa calls me his special version of my given name, Willanne—unlike my cousins, who call me "Pudgy." I am pudgy, as pictures thirty years later attest. But today I am four and I don't care if I'm "Pudgy," because Grandpa loves me best. I don't know how I know this, I just know, that's all.

I remember.

I am eleven. We are visiting Grandma's house and my detestable cousins have a friend over. My cousins are running around under the umbrella tree in the front yard and shrieking brainlessly. But their friend—a boy—is not running and shrieking. My cousins are gleefully teasing him, daring him to kiss me. I hate my cousins. My horrible cousins still call me "Pudgy," though I've outgrown the appropriateness of the name. I'm so embarrassed.

I remember.

I am sixteen. I pass the driving test easily, both the written and the driving portion. But the hard question comes after "Sex," "Color of eyes" and "Height." The question is: "Weight." How much should I say, I wonder. What happens if I lie? Will I have to step on a scale? If I lie will an alarm go off? Will the clerk repeat my weight out loud so everyone will know? Will she question me? Will she exclaim disbelievingly, "You weigh how much?" Filled with trepidation, I decide to lie. I wonder how much I can get away with. I take off ten pounds. I get away with it. No alarm sounds. The clerk doesn't even raise an eyebrow. She acts like she doesn't even care, though I'm sure she must.

I get away with my first ten-pound lie: Ten pounds becomes my permanent cheat number. No matter how much I weigh, from then on, I always take off ten pounds before committing my weight to paper. And I always know — no matter how much I weigh — that if I just lose ten pounds, I'll be just right. No matter how much I weigh, "just right" is always ten pounds less.

In the suburban morning quiet, I remember.

Six years ago, I was pregnant and looking like the Goodyear blimp. But today I am thirty-four, and I'm not pregnant. I'm also not fat. I'm not even pudgy. But the scale has just pronounced judgment and destroyed my mood by telling me I gained a pound.

I contemplate this: Maybe how much I weigh is not the problem; perhaps the problem is how I feel about how much I weigh.

Unhurried, I rise from the bed to which the bathroom scale has so recently sent me. I put on my robe, and go to the bathroom. I pick up the scale and carry it deliberately down the hall, past the dining room, through the kitchen, to the side yard where six empty trash cans await next week's trash. I raise the scale to the level of my shoulders, pause for just a moment and then drop the mechanical dictator into the waiting rubbish receptacle. And in so doing, I reclaim control over my own morale.

Never again will my mood be determined by the bathroom scale. A happy birthday belongs to me.

~Willanne Ackerman
Chicken Soup for the Unsinkable Soul

32

A Real Home

Attitude is a little thing that makes a big difference.
~Winston Churchill

Her world had shattered with the divorce.

Bills, house payments, health insurance. Her part-time job provided little income and fewer benefits. With no financial support, she had finally lost the house.

At wit's end, Karen managed to rent a cramped camper at the local RV park for herself and five-year-old Joshua. It was only a little better than living in their car, and she wished with all her heart that she could provide more for her child.

After their evening ritual of giggling over a table game and reading stories, Karen sent her son outside to play until bedtime while she agonized over the checkbook. She glanced out the window when she heard voices.

"Say, Josh, don't you wish you had a real home?" asked the campground manager.

Karen tensed and held her breath as she leaned nearer the open window. Then a smile spread across her face when she heard Joshua's response.

"We already have a real home," he said. "It's just that we don't have a house to put it in."

~Carol McAdoo Rehme
Chicken Soup for the Mother's Soul 2

Fear and Cheer

I made my resolution at my daughter's National Cheerleading Competition in Disney World. It was a surprising place for me to make a resolution, given Disney, cheerleading, and me are an unlikely combination. I am always more concerned with finding a yoga class and a pretty place to run. In contrast, my daughter had been eagerly anticipating this trip for months — training, stretching, and tumbling with the discipline of an Olympian. "And the rides Mom, now that will be great!"

Great wasn't the first word that came to mind when I thought about roller coasters in the dark and elevators crashing from the sky. But it was that kid-like sparkle in her brown eyes which was the first glimmer of my resolution. I'd always been terrified of scary rides — safely watching, holding my children's melting ice cream as they danced in the sky high above. Their laughter and excitement was a joy to watch, but sharing it would be even better. So as my daughter hoped to return with a national award, I wanted to return having championed my fear. She was training to do flips in the air and I was preparing to fly — holding on for dear life.

All cheerleaders had to be accompanied by a parent chaperone, and compared to my husband, I'm a pom-pom professional. We attended numerous meetings with coaches where we were handed lists, competition schedules, bus schedules, lodging specifics, and rule sheets as we prepared for the launch of two hundred cheerleaders. I'd do my best to be a good cheerleading mom but I also knew I was going to lead a silent cheer for myself that wasn't written on any of the handouts.

I tried to be organized for our adventure, buying my Disney ticket on-line. Unfortunately I proudly purchased a three-day pass to Disneyland in California instead of Disney World in Florida. The smiley woman at guest relations shook her head, apologized and politely handed it back to me. "Y'all will just have to buy a new $250 pass." And then… "All righty, I'll give you a complimentary ticket, but shush now and just keep yourselves movin'." Her small gesture was like a fortune cookie message, "Resolutions can cost nothing, but be worth everything." She suddenly looked enchanting and the Magic Kingdom—just magical.

We spent the weekend in a "clump"—four daughters and four mothers, busing it between competitions. My daughter lives her fourteen-year-old life in a clump, a group project with her friends that is devoted to growing up all too quickly. In contrast I have dear friends but have always appreciated my solitude. Group travel isn't usually my chosen form of transportation. So along with roller coasters and elevators that drop from the sky, I was confronting my shyness in a group of moms, among an even larger group of tourists, bumping elbows, all searching for the electrifying thrill of Disney.

Since it was a freezing weekend in Orlando, I did have to purchase two pairs of Mickey socks to wear with my sandals, which got a few looks from my daughter. But she often finds me embarrassing these days; Mickey socks are the least of it.

But the true warmth came from spending time with the other mothers. Quickly, we stopped talking about the weather, and began sharing our lives, loves, losses, heartaches and laughter. They were patient with me, as I tend to ask curious questions both in and out of my psychotherapy office. My mother always reminds me that at age four I asked a divorced neighbor, "Exactly what didn't you like about your first husband?" Trailing behind four adolescent jabbering girls with large red and blue bows in their hair was contagious. We mothers began to wonder if we'd soon be texting each other, sipping from the same straw and borrowing clothes.

Given that the girls spend much of their lives "getting ready," we all found ourselves stumbling towards our toothbrushes at 5:30 A.M.—preparing for the 7:00 bus launch, with the coach refrain in our head, "DON'T EVER, EVER BE LATE!" With the end of the competition, the girls made us all proud. But for me, my biggest challenge was just beginning. We all "clumped" together to plan our afternoon rides. I found myself saying, "You know I could always sit with a cup of tea and my book." My new friends laughed, letting me know there would be no back door at Disney.

I had already decided that I would need a way to manage my anxiety. I began to think of those moments in yoga class when the soft voice of my teacher guides us through a meditation. I find that place inside where for a moment the world is truly peaceful. I asked my daughter if she'd sit next to me on the elevator ride that drops from the sky. How many nights had she come running in, in the dark, whispering, "Mommy, I'm scared." And now it is my turn to rely on my grown-up daughter. We buckled up laughing and screaming before the ride even began. I tried to breathe in and out and find that yoga place, depending on both myself and my small community to keep me safe. And suddenly WHOOOOSH! We were dropping, shrieking and holding each other tight.

The exhilaration left me tearful and with that childlike feeling of, "Again Mommy, again."

Of course, we did celebrate with another time high in the sky. But the true celebration was getting on board with some dear friends and "clumping it." I learned to rely on strangers who had become friends, reminding me that group travel provides a smoother ride in this wild and spinning world. One resolution has led me to another, which is to risk leaning on others more, because it gives us all the chance to fly. And that is something we can cheer for.

~Priscilla Dann-Courtney
Chicken Soup for the Soul: My Resolution

34

A Matter of Weight

Ever since grade school, when being the biggest girl in class landed me more than a fair share of snickers, I've had a difficult relationship with my weight. Kids called me all sorts of names—Pork Ball, Porcupine Rind, Jam Pudding and worse. I pretended to laugh along with them, but went home and drowned my anger in food.

It wasn't until I turned eighteen and fell in love with a tall, soft-spoken boy from Massachusetts that the weight slipped off. And when I married him six years later, I was a svelte 103 pounds. For someone who enjoyed food as much as I did, this was no small feat. Those were the Twiggy days, when being knitting-needle thin had become a cultural obsession; the fashion industry was relentlessly unforgiving towards natural bulges and buxom shapes.

But "skinny" didn't last long. Within two years, I gained over ten pounds, and with the birth of our first child three years later, I added another forty. The old grade school angst returned, and I decided to wage my own holy war against the bulge. I took up running, beginning with a brisk walk around the block, and then doubled my efforts until I was able to run comfortably for two miles without stopping. By the end of the year, I had shed thirty pounds and was permanently hooked on running. It made me feel brisk and clean, like a colt; it allowed me to eat what I wanted and it kept the weight manageable.

As long as I pounded the pavement for fifty minutes, five times a week, I was able to keep my weight within an acceptable range.

Still, I fretted over every bite. My husband, much more relaxed about body shape, said, "I wish you could just enjoy being what you are. You carry so much guilt about what you do and what you look like that you aren't enjoying life at all!"

"But I feel so fat!" I countered.

"I have a suggestion. Get rid of your scale."

I did — and miraculously discovered that my body had its own way of finding balance. I moved from "how much I weigh" to "how I feel." For several years, I ate when I was hungry and ran not because I had to, but simply because I loved the sense of exhilaration it gave me. I didn't choose one activity to cancel out the other, but did both because they fed my soul. And although I didn't know exactly how much I weighed, I was content because my clothes remained a comfortable fit.

Then everything changed the year I turned fifty. My husband passed away after an eleven-month battle with cancer. Food became a different kind of issue during his illness, when his body refused to eat because the radiation had scorched his throat and he couldn't swallow without pain. Day by day, I watched him shrink to a shadow.

After his death, I was plagued by a terrible loneliness. In the silence of an empty home, I ate, wept and ate again. I noticed my body becoming dumpy and thick. Despite a daily run, pockets of flesh flapped under my arms and my belly jiggled like Jell-O. A year later, my obsession with weight returned.

I bought a new scale, joined the local fitness club, placed myself on a high-protein diet and squelched my natural enjoyment of food. I ate only what was permitted: egg whites, cheese, onions, tofu, seeds, nuts and lentils, and drank designer whey drinks. I ran six days a week and did an hour of resistance training three times a week. I worked out this way for four weeks, like a soldier, then I stepped on the scale. You could have heard my scream ten miles down the road: I had gained three pounds. How was that possible?

An older friend had once said, "You just wait — the day will come when your body will stop performing for you. It will bloat, swell and gurgle; it will rise and spread and do all the nasty things you exercise freaks are trying to keep under control. Just wait and see." Her eyes gleamed with venom.

I would have believed her and turned the rest of my life into a lament had it not been for a vivid dream, which came like a message from my body:

I was on a dark, stuffy train. Several people were with me, and we were on a mission of some kind. They had wrapped me up in long sheets and placed me in the aisle. When the train stopped, the sheets peeled off, and I followed the crowd out the gates and down winding stairs towards some kind of underground cavern. The journey was long and tedious, but we finally emerged from the last flight of stairs into the depths of a cave. There, in the center, was my husband, lying on a hospital bed. He was bone-thin, cheeks sunken, eyes hollow. I walked up to him, placed my hand over my hip and complained to him, "I can't stand it. All this work coming down here and I haven't lost a pound."

Then I woke up, and it hit me: that dream showed the absurd irony of my situation. My husband could barely eat at all, and all I could think about was losing weight.

The next morning I threw away the scale.

Life, I decided, was too short for weights and measures. I would run and I would eat. I would take pleasure in both. I would neither deny my body nor starve my soul. I was going to love my body in whatever shape and form it took. My body was here to serve a higher purpose, my soul's purpose, and my soul was not here to be shaped or stuffed into a standard mold.

~Mary Desaulniers
Chicken Soup to Inspire the Body and Soul

Woman to Woman

Overcoming Obstacles

You cannot discover new oceans
unless you have the courage to lose sight of the shore.
~Author Unknown

35

A Day at The Tradition

Laughter is the shortest distance between two people.
~Victor Borge

Several years ago, I was diagnosed with cancer. It was the most difficult time I have ever faced. I think it was my sense of humor that allowed me to hold onto my sanity. Like many people who have gone through chemotherapy, I lost all of my hair and I was as bald as a cue ball. I always had enjoyed wearing hats, so when my hair deserted me, I ordered several special hats with the hair already attached. It was easy and I never had to worry about how my hair looked.

I have always been a big golf fan. In fact, I have been to twenty-three straight U.S. Opens. At one point during my cancer treatments, my husband John and I decided to get away from the cold Minnesota winter and took a trip to Scottsdale, Arizona. There was a Senior PGA Tour event called The Tradition being played, and that seemed like just the ticket to lift my spirits.

The first day of the tournament brought out a huge gallery. It was a beautiful day, and I was in heaven. I was standing just off the third tee, behind the fairway ropes, watching my three favorite golfers in the world approach the tee box: Jack Nicklaus, Raymond Floyd and Tom Weiskopf.

Just as they arrived at the tee, the unimaginable happened. A huge gust of wind came up from nowhere and blew my hat and hair right off my head and into the middle of the fairway! The thousands of spectators lining the fairway fell into an awkward silence, all eyes on me. Even my golf idols were watching me, as my hair was in their flight path. I was mortified! Embarrassed as I was, I knew I couldn't just stand there. Someone had to do something to get things moving again.

So I took a deep breath, went under the ropes and out into the middle of the fairway. I grabbed my hat and hair, nestled them back on my head as best I could. Then I turned to the golfers and loudly announced, "Gentlemen, the wind is blowing from left to right."

They say the laughter could be heard all the way to the nineteenth hole.

~Christine Clifford
Chicken Soup for the Golfer's Soul

Cultivating My Garden

The greatest gift of the garden is the restoration of the five senses.
~Hanna Rion

It was a summer's evening when my husband Tim's minivan spun out of control on a rain-slicked road, leaving me a young widow with a little daughter to raise.

On a fall day three months later, as I struggled to work through the grief, the pain and even the anger, I stood on the back steps of my house, surveying the large vegetable garden that Tim had put so much of himself into. From the yard, my eyes wandered over to the wooded slope beyond it and to the cemetery where Tim was buried, and then back to the garden.

The garden was a mess. I couldn't possibly keep up with it all. I didn't even know where to begin. The bright, green-bean wall Tim had constructed was covered with rotting beans, and every other green growing thing had been choked out by the ornamental gourds we had mistakenly planted last spring. What was I to do with it all? I certainly didn't want to turn it back into the sort of manicured greenery that both Tim and I had always loathed.

After much pondering, I decided to make an herb garden out of it. Something that I could lose myself in.

The bean wall came down and was hauled to the town dump. I closed my heart to the memory of the warm late-spring morning when Tim had been up early, painting it gaudy green, and threw myself into ripping down the ragged sunflowers and sadly faded cosmos he had planted all along the edges.

Then came the herbs. Lamb's ears, rosemary, angelica and costmary. Lavender, speedwell, lemon balm and valerian. Spearmint, apple mint and—would you believe?—chocolate mint.

In the strawberry bed that Tim had made for me the second Mother's Day after our daughter Marissa was born, I planted a white birch. Well, it was gray just then, but Eric, one of my garden wizards, told me that it would turn white some day. It became the Tim Tree.

In the spring, with the help of my friend Cel, I put down wood chips. Another friend, Jan, went on an herb shopping trip and came over with plants I'd never seen or even heard of, with names like woad, soapwort, felicity, amaranth and woundwort.

The garden was taking shape all right. But I still felt lost and unhappy in my own skin. I toyed with the idea of selling the house and moving with Marissa into my grandmother's old farmhouse. There would be no memories of Tim to gnaw at me there.

But I still kept puttering with that garden. I moved the white marble birdbath that Tim had given me on our last anniversary into the center. I bought a stone angel, her eyes downcast and her face filled with Renaissance piety, and placed her next to the birdbath.

Still, it seemed that something was missing. Then it occurred to me that my garden had no central theme. I had always been fascinated by "theme gardens"—Shakespearean gardens, moonlight gardens, witches' gardens and the like. But mine was simply a hodgepodge of herbs, flowers, trees and shrubs.

Late that summer, Marissa and I traveled to New York State. We stopped at an herb farm, and I came across some new herbs with bewitching names, such as boneset and all-heal. Boneset leaves, I learned, were originally used in setting broken bones and in tonics. All-heal, or self-heal, was a remedy for a variety of internal and external wounds. It was then that I decided that my garden would be a healing garden. Not only in the literal sense, but perhaps in the spiritual sense as well.

One afternoon not long afterwards, I stumbled right smack

into my epiphany. I had fallen in love with my garden. My bane had turned out to be my blessing. I gazed around me, just as I had the previous fall, but with such different eyes. The garden had made me remember what I had tried so hard to forget: that I loved this place where Tim and I had started our journey as husband and wife and as parents of a vivacious daughter. That part of the journey was over, but the journey continued. Marissa and I still had miles to go and promises to keep—to each other, to Tim and to the garden. We'd make good where we were.

Over a year later, I'm still working at my garden. I've moved the trees out and put a tiny iris garden in one corner. And I've been putting down flat bricks, fieldstone, and anything else I can lay my hands on, to make little wayward paths that branch out, then circle back on themselves. Sometimes I just sit on the marble bench that I put in, and at other times I hunt around for the four- and five-leaved clovers that often crop up, good luck signs that assure me nature is working for me.

I don't go down to the cemetery much now. If I want to find Tim, I feel him in this garden he gave me. The pain has gone from my memories now, leaving them full of laughter and warmth. The healing garden has lived up to its name.

~T. J. Banks
Chicken Soup for the Single's Soul

A Lesson from Luke

One bright, sunny afternoon in September our golden retriever, Luke, rose from a nap to go for our usual walk to the park. I should say he attempted to rise, because as he stood, he wobbled, tried to get his balance, then collapsed. My heart did somersaults as my husband and I carried him to the car and sped to the vet's office. After hours of blood tests, exams and an ultrasound, we learned the grim news: Luke had hemangiosarcoma, an inoperable cancer of the blood vessels.

"How long does he have?" I asked through my tears, my arms wrapped around Luke, hugging him to my heart.

"I can't say for sure," the vet told us. "Weeks. Maybe only days."

I barely made it to the car before I broke down in uncontrollable sobs. My husband didn't handle the news any better. We held on to each other and bawled. How could Luke have gotten so sick without our realizing it? Sure, he was ten years old, but you'd never know it. He ate every meal with the gusto of a starving piglet, and just that morning he'd chased his tennis ball as if it were filled with his favorite doggy biscuits. He couldn't have cancer, not our Luker Boy, not our baby.

For the next several days we hovered over him, studying him diligently. We took slow walks around the neighborhood, and instead of throwing the ball, we tossed it right to his mouth and let him catch it. One day while dusting the furniture, I picked up his blue pet-therapist vest—Luke had been a volunteer with the Helen Woodward Animal Center pet therapy department, and had visited centers for abused and neglected children. I held the vest to my cheek and started to cry. Why Luke? He was such a sweet dog; he deserved to live.

As I started to put the vest away in a drawer, Luke trotted over, wagging his tail. He looked at me expectantly, his ears perked up and his tongue hanging out.

"You want to put on your vest and go to work, don't you?" I knelt and scratched behind his ears. I could swear he grinned at me.

Although there could be no running or jumping, the following day Luke joined the other pet-therapy dogs on a visit to the children's center. I'm often envious of Luke's ability to light up kids' faces just by being himself. They giggle and clap their hands when he gives them a high ten or catches a cookie off his nose. But the best reaction by far comes when the children ask him, "Do you love me?" and he answers with an emphatic, "Woof!" The kids whoop and holler, continuing to shout, "Do you love me?" He always answers them.

On this particular day, I wanted to make sure that Luke enjoyed himself, so I wasn't paying as much attention to the children as I usually did. A girl about nine or ten years old inched over to us. Her narrow shoulders slumped and her head hung down; she reminded me of a drooping sunflower. Luke wagged his tail as she neared us and licked her cheek when she bent to pet him. She sat next to us on the lawn and smiled at Luke, but her large brown eyes still looked sad.

"I wish people would die at ten years old the way dogs do," she said.

Stunned, I could only stare at her. None of the kids knew that Luke had cancer. Luke rolled over on his back and the girl rubbed his belly.

Finally, I asked her, "Why do you say that?"

"Because I'm ten, and I wish I would die."

Her sorrow curled around my heart and squeezed it so tightly, my breath caught. "Are things so bad?"

"The worst. I hate it here."

What could I say to her? I couldn't tell her that she shouldn't feel that way, or that she had a wonderful life ahead of her. What good would that do? It wasn't what she needed to hear. I put my hand gently on her back and asked her name.

"Carly."

"Carly, you want to know something? Luke here has cancer. He's dying. And he wishes more than anything that he could go on living. You're perfectly healthy, yet you want to die. It just isn't fair, is it?"

Carly snapped her head up and looked at me. "Luke's dying?"

I nodded, swallowing back tears. "He doesn't have much time — a week, maybe two... or just a few days... we don't know for sure."

"Shouldn't he be at home or in the hospital?" she asked.

"He wanted to visit with you kids, to bring you some happiness. Just like you, things aren't good for him either. He probably hurts a lot inside." I paused, wondering if she was old enough to understand. "But by coming here, it's as if he's trying to make every minute of his life count for something."

Carly sat silently, looking at Luke while she softly rubbed his belly. "Poor Luke," she said, almost in a whisper. When she raised her head and met my gaze, her eyes looked wary, almost accusing. "You think I should be glad I'm alive and not wanting to die, don't you? Even if I'm stuck here."

I took a few seconds to try to gather my thoughts. "Maybe you could make it sort of like a game. Every day try to think of at least one good thing about being alive."

The counselors began calling the children back to their class-rooms. I looked straight into Carly's eyes, trying to reach her. "If nothing else, there's always hope things will get better."

"Come on, Carly," a counselor called out.

Carly stood. "Will you come back and see me?"

"Yes, I will. I promise. And you'll tell me lots of reasons to live, right?"

"Right." She gave me a big nod, and then ran off to join her classmates.

The next week, though Luke's walk was slower and more labored, we visited the children's center again. Carly didn't show up. Alarmed, I asked one of the counselors where she was. They told me that she'd gone to live with a foster family. My heart settled back into place. Good for you, Carly.

Twelve days later, Luke lost his battle with cancer.

When I think of him now, I try to focus on what I told Carly: that Luke made every minute of his life count for something. Perhaps he inspired Carly to do that, too. I hope that she, and all the other children we visited, benefited from being with Luke. I know I did.

~Christine Watkins
Chicken Soup for the Dog Lover's Soul

A Little White Lie

Friends are relatives you make for yourself.
~Eustache Deschamps

When my friend, Sadie, was taken to the emergency room at a local hospital, I rushed over to be with her as soon as I received the news.

Sadie was both surprised and pleased to see me. "How did you get them to let you in?" she asked, knowing visitors were not usually allowed in the emergency room.

I, too, had been concerned about that on the drive over. However, I knew Sadie needed a friend to comfort her. In desperation, I had decided if worse came to worst, I would be forced to tell a lie and say I was Sadie's sister. I hoped I wouldn't have to resort to that.

After I explained all this to Sadie, she threw back her head in hearty laughter. While I was trying to figure out why Sadie was laughing, I glanced down at our clasped hands—my very white one held gently between her two black ones.

~June Cerza Kolf
Chicken Soup for the Sister's Soul

Wigged Out!

"So," my oncologist's nurse continued, handing me a list of names and addresses, "you may want to check one of these out."

Glancing at the sheet, I caught my breath: "Stores Specializing in Wigs for Chemo Patients."

Chemo. I still could hardly bring myself to accept the word. Numbly, I headed for one of the wig stores on the list. Inwardly I seethed. Not fair, God. You know I hate wigs. Last time I wore one was in the seventies. Loathed it. I looked like something in a B-movie. No, make that a D-one. Surely You don't want me to look like that!

Stepping into the little shop, I felt even worse. Almost every inch was filled with row upon row of artificial heads with artificial smiles topped with artificial hair.

The shop owner's smile, though, was warm and real. An older Asian woman, she tried to put me at ease. She picked out a few of her treasures that seemed closest in style, length and color to mine, then tried them on me. She expertly flipped the shiny locks this way and that, showing me how easily they could be arranged and cared for.

I had to admit that things had improved since the seventies. But I still rebelled. I liked to be natural, real, unpretentious. Wigs were so not me. Period.

Just then, an older gentleman came in, wearing a smile, golf togs and a glowing head of white hair. What in the world was he doing here?

"Hi, again," he greeted the shop owner. "I'm ready for a new wig. This one's fine, but I'd like an extra on hand. What have you got in stock?"

Smiling at me, he said, "These little things sure are a bother, but for us chemo patients, they're worth their weight in gold." Chemo patient? Him?

He gave me a thumbs-up. "Don't let it get you down, dear. We're all in this together."

Just then a tall, well-built younger woman breezed in. Her cap of glowing red curls caught my eye, but what really lit up that little shop was her vibrant smile. Perfect picture of health!

"I'm back!" she announced. "I really liked the one I had last year. Got any more in red?" Then to me, "You'll like shopping here. Started chemo already?"

"No, uh, will you be having it too?"

She laughed. "Oh, I'm an old-timer at this. Went through the whole business, lost all my hair. Took a year to grow it back. I was so thrilled to see it again." She wistfully touched one of her curls. "But now they've found a tumor somewhere else. So I'm going on Taxol. Hello, chemo, bye-bye, hair." Laughing, she continued. "Oh, but it is just hair, isn't it? After all, hair can always come back. Life can't."

Tears stung my eyes. "You are so right," I said. "Here, let me help you find what you need." And suddenly we were sisters, laughing and chatting together as I picked a wig out and tried it on her. Perfect!

The storekeeper wrote all three of our names down in a simple spiral-bound notebook, following hundreds of others. "This is my prayer book," she said simply. "I pray for all my customers, in chemo and out. I'll pray for all of you, too, that God will be with you and help you."

That little shop was still crowded, shabby and dark. But suddenly it was filled with light and joy as we all hugged each other. Yes, our newly purchased hairpieces were artificial. But our newfound hope and love as instant friends and supporters was real.

~Bonnie Compton Hanson
Chicken Soup for the Christian Woman's Soul

Woman to Woman

Achieving Your Dream

Don't be afraid to go out on a limb. That's where the fruit is.
~Janie Mines

40

Women Are Persons!

It was we, the people; not we, the white male citizens;
nor yet we, the male citizens;
but we, the whole people, who formed the Union....
Men, their rights and nothing more;
women, their rights and nothing less.
~Susan B. Anthony

Judge Emily Murphy was frustrated. Her last petition had been no more successful than all the others she had sent over the past ten years. It was 1927, and Canadian women were still defined by British common law, which astonishingly stated: "Women are persons in matters of pains and penalties, but not in matters of rights and privileges."

Emily was not at all happy about the outrageous indignity of being told she was "not a person." She had set her sights on becoming Canada's first female senator, but because women were not "persons," no woman was eligible! Emily was determined to change things.

And so it was that between 1921 and 1927, over 500,000 people, men and women, had signed letters and petitions requesting that Judge Murphy be appointed to the Canadian Senate. For most of them, it wasn't about becoming a senator. Like her, they were upset and offended that women were not considered to be persons. Amazingly, despite all her efforts, two prime ministers had still said "no!" But Emily refused to take "no" for an answer and kept up her relentless pressure. Then one day, after ten years of lobbying, she happened upon a new strategy.

Her brother had discovered a legal clause stating that any five citizens acting as a unit could appeal to the Supreme Court to clarify a point in the constitution. So in late 1927, she invited Henrietta Edwards, Louise McKinney, Irene Parlby and Nellie McClung to her Edmonton home. All four of these prominent Alberta women had been active in fighting for women's rights, and all of them were determined that by the end of their efforts, Canada would recognize them and all women as "persons."

That day, the five women signed Emily's petition, and with great hopes and expectations they sent their appeal. Then they sat back and waited. Several months later, Judge Murphy excitedly opened the telegram that arrived from the Supreme Court of Canada.

But her hopes were dashed. "No," read the reply from the learned justices, "Women are not eligible to be summoned to the Senate. Women are not 'persons.'"

Emily and her colleagues were devastated. First two prime ministers, and now the highest court in Canada had formally ruled against them, and they feared they had done irreparable damage to their cause. However, further research revealed one more option. The absolute final court for Canada in those days was still the Privy Council of Great Britain—it could be appealed there. But they were not hopeful. They would have to persuade the Canadian government to appeal the decision, and the rights of women in England were far behind those so far gained in Canada.

Holding her breath, Emily wrote to Prime Minister Mackenzie King, asked for his support, and urged him to appeal this matter to the Privy Council. To her great elation, he responded with his full support, and that of his government, and in addition they would pay for the cost of the appeal!

With their hopes back up, the five women wondered, Should they go to England? Should they write articles for the newspapers? Contact their friends there? No, they were advised, only the merit of the case would be heard. Just wait.

Finally, in October 1929, the five British Lords made their historic decision. When Emily and her friends learned that the new definition of the word "persons" would from that day forward always include both men and women, they were overjoyed! They had won!

As the word spread, women around the world celebrated. The five friends were gratified to know that because of their efforts, every woman in the British Empire would now be recognized as a "person," with all the same rights and privileges as men.

[Editors' Note: On October 18, 2000, a memorial celebrating the Famous 5 and their tremendous accomplishments was unveiled, and our five heroes became the first Canadian women in history to be honoured on Parliament Hill. The monument depicts an imaginary moment when the women received the news of their victory. A joyous Emily stands beside an empty chair and beckons visitors to join the celebration. Today, many come and visit so they can sit in Emily's chair and thank the Famous 5 for what they did. And everyone who does makes a pledge to do their best to participate in the building of a better Canada!]

~Frances Wright
Chicken Soup for the Canadian Soul

$\mathcal{D}$are to $\mathcal{I}$magine

Don't live down to expectations. Go out there and do something remarkable.
~Wendy Wasserstein

When people find out that I competed in the Olympics, they assume I've always been an accomplished athlete. But it isn't true. I was not the strongest, or the fastest, and I didn't learn the quickest. For me, becoming an Olympian was not developing a gift of natural athletic ability, but was, literally, an act of will.

At the 1972 Olympics in Munich, I was a member of the U.S. pentathlon team, but the tragedy of the Israeli athletes and an injury to my ankle combined to make the experience a deeply discouraging one. I didn't quit; instead I kept training, eventually qualifying to go with the U.S. team to Montreal for the 1976 Games. The experience was much more joyous, and I was thrilled to place thirteenth. But still, I felt I could do better.

I arranged to take a leave of absence from my college coaching job the year before the 1980 Olympics. I figured that twelve months of "twenty-four-hour-a-day training" would give me the edge I needed to bring home a medal this time. In the summer of 1979, I started intensively training for the Olympic trials to be held in June of 1980. I felt the exhilaration that comes with single-minded focus and steady progress towards a cherished goal.

But then in November, what appeared to be an insurmountable

obstacle occurred. I was in a car accident and injured my lower back. The doctors weren't sure exactly what was wrong, but I had to stop training because I couldn't move without experiencing excruciating pain. It seemed all too obvious that I would have to give up my dream of going to the Olympics if I couldn't keep training. Everyone felt so sorry for me. Everyone but me.

It was strange, but I never believed this setback would stop me. I trusted that the doctors and physical therapists would get it handled soon, and I would get back to training. I held on to the affirmation: I'm getting better every day and I will place in the top three at the Olympic trials. It went through my head constantly.

But my progress was slow, and the doctors couldn't agree on a course of treatment. Time was passing, and I was still in pain, unable to move. With only a few months remaining, I had to do something or I knew I would never make it. So I started training the only way I could—in my head.

A pentathlon consists of five track and field events: the 100-meter hurdle, the shot put, the high jump, the long jump and the 200-meter sprint. I obtained films of the world-record holders in all five of my events. Sitting in a kitchen chair, I watched the films projected on my kitchen wall over and over. Sometimes, I watched them in slow motion or frame by frame. When I got bored, I watched them backwards, just for fun. I watched for hundreds of hours, studying and absorbing. Other times, I lay on the couch and visualized the experience of competing in minute detail. I know some people thought I was crazy, but I wasn't ready to give up yet. I trained as hard as I could—without ever moving a muscle.

Finally, the doctors diagnosed my problem as a bulging disc. Now I knew why I was in agony when I moved, but I still couldn't train. Later, when I could walk a little, I went to the track and had them set up all five of my events. Even though I couldn't practice, I would stand on the track and envision in my mind the complete physical training routine I would have gone through that day if I had been able. For months, I repeatedly imagined myself competing and qualifying at the trials.

But was visualizing enough? Was it truly possible that I could place in the top three at the Olympic trials? I believed it with all my heart.

By the time the trials actually rolled around, I had healed just enough to compete. Being very careful to keep my muscles and tendons warm, I moved through my five events as if in a dream. Afterwards, as I walked across the field, I heard a voice on the loudspeaker announcing my name.

It took my breath away, even though I had imagined it a thousand times in my mind. I felt a wave of pure joy wash over me as the announcer said, "Second place, 1980 Olympic Pentathlon: Marilyn King."

~Marilyn King as told to Carol Kline
Chicken Soup for the Unsinkable Soul

42

Give It a Try

Shoot for the moon. Even if you miss, you'll land among the stars.
~Les Brown

I love the kids of Hawai'i. I enjoyed being one, and I enjoyed teaching them. So it was fitting that I ended up teaching and coaching at Holy Family Catholic Academy, the same school I attended as a junior high student.

One day in October 1999, two eighth grade girls on my volleyball team, Rachael and Emerisa, came to talk with me. "Coach Angie," they said, "now that the volleyball season is over and this is our last year at Holy Family, we'd really like to try out for the basketball team. But we've never played basketball before, and we'll be embarrassed if the younger players make the team and we don't."

"You're both talented and athletic," I started. "If you don't try, you'll never know." Hoping to convince them, I said, "If you're willing to try, I'll help you prepare for tryouts." I noticed in their faces that they were still reluctant to accept the challenge.

As a coach and teacher, I love to inspire my students to accomplish more than they think they can. So I tried to encourage them with my own story. I told the girls how I'd twice competed and lost in the local and state preliminary pageants to Miss America back when I was just eighteen and nineteen years old. "You win something even if you lose," I told them. "Even though I didn't win the state competitions, I gained self-confidence and honed my communication skills.

I also earned thousands in scholarship assistance. It's always worth it to try." The girls said they'd think about it, and went home.

The next day, Rachael and Emerisa surprisingly agreed to my plan. But there was a catch. "Okay, Coach Angie," they said. "We'll get ready with you for basketball tryouts, only if you'll compete again for Miss America."

"What?" I said in shock. "I was just a teenager then. I've got a job now!"

They looked at each other. "But, you still have one last year to try, just like us! Are you scared?" one asked.

"Don't you want to face and overcome your fear?" asked the other, trying to look angelic and keep a straight face at the same time.

I almost had to laugh. They caught me at my own lesson.

As I went home that night, I thought, How can I talk "the talk" if I don't live it myself? I have to show them I mean what I say.

The next day I went back and agreed to their bargain.

So the girls started practicing basketball, and I once again began honing my public speaking and pageant skills, while continuing to teach and coach at the school.

The night I competed for Miss O'ahu in January 2000, Rachael and Emerisa were in the audience screaming for me. When I was named first runner-up, they both beamed with pride. Even though I was not the winner, I knew I had just displayed courage and taught them that you never know what you can do until you try.

"You came so close!" said Rachael.

"If you try again, I'll bet you can win!" said Emerisa.

Their enthusiasm spurred me to overcome my fears and challenge myself to try one last preliminary pageant—Miss Leeward. It was my very last chance to run in the Miss America system, and this time, I won.

I advanced to the state level and became Miss Hawai'i in June 2000. As one of the fifty-one contestants in the national pageant, a full crew came to Hawai'i to film my students and the youth choir I direct. This became my motivation and my lucky charm. During the actual week of national competition, I didn't have time to be nervous because my focus was just to make the top ten so that my kids would get to see themselves on television! Again, my students had propelled me to do my best and be a role model for them.

Then, on October 14, 2000, I was crowned the first teacher and first Asian to become Miss America in the pageant's eighty-year history.

It was such a blessing to finally realize a dream I thought was once out of reach. I got to travel across the country, talking to thousands of people about my platform of character education in the classrooms, valuing our nation's teachers and about my beautiful Hawai'i.

And the icing on the cake?

Rachael and Emerisa not only made the basketball team; they became team captains.

As my students have taught me, it's always worth it to try.

~Angela Perez Baraquiro
Chicken Soup for the Soul of Hawaii

A Long Hot Summer

Success isn't a result of spontaneous combustion.
You must set yourself on fire.
~Arnold H. Glasow

There are numerous reasons why a middle-aged woman who has been away from the workforce rearing her children decides to go back to work. The obvious might be for money, but that was not my reason.

After my children departed for college, perhaps I was just bored, or possibly I was suffering from the empty nest syndrome, but in actuality I think I decided to return to work because I was just plain hot. Colorado was experiencing an extremely hot, dry summer and my home lacked air conditioning. It was hot, and I was hot. I determined a cool air conditioned office was where I belonged! Years ago my first job was that of a bookkeeper—it was then that I worked for money. While my children were growing up I worked part time in the school system as a teacher's aide.

This time around I wanted to do something different, something new and exciting, and the money wasn't too important, as my husband made a very comfortable living for us. But what should I do? What sort of job should I look for? I knew I needed to be cautious as to what I became involved with. I am not a "quitter" and therefore I hoped to avoid becoming obligated to an employer in a job that might turn out to be a mistake for me.

A Long Hot Summer: Achieving Your Dream   147

While I agonized over what to do, I was reminded of a past incident where I needed to replace my original engagement ring as the gold was wearing thin. My husband and I shopped and shopped for one, everywhere we went, even when we were on vacation. Finally this nonstop searching prompted my poor husband to ask, "Just what kind of ring do you want, what exactly are we looking for?"

My reply was, "I honestly don't know, but when I see the correct setting, I will know it." That was the way I felt about the new career I wished to pursue; I didn't have a clue as to what I wanted to do, but knew there was a perfect fit for me, if I would just be patient.

Fortunately, that summer while attending my twenty-fifth high school class reunion, I overheard a former classmate describing what she did for a living. She was a travel agent, and she and her husband had just returned from a trip to Hawaii where they acted as chaperones for a group of travelers. WOW, that sounded like fun, considerably more fun and exciting than being a bookkeeper. Apparently this profession also had some great travel benefits. I innocently pondered the idea of becoming a travel agent. After all, how difficult could it be to write airline tickets and plan vacations? I reasoned if my friend could do it, I probably could, too, and after all, "I love to travel." I later learned uttering the phrase, "I love to travel", is a surefire way to prevent you from being hired when applying for a job in the travel industry. That phrase is definitely a no-no!

BINGO! It was as if fireworks lit up the night sky! Right then and there I knew without a doubt, I had found the perfect fit; I wanted to be a travel agent. Little did I realize travel agents are a specialized group of individuals whose work is both stressful and demanding. Theirs is a profession requiring special education, training and experience to become proficient. There is definitely more to it than meets the eye. There is unquestionably more to it than just generating airline tickets.

I began scanning the "help wanted" ads in my local newspaper and quickly discovered agencies were interested in hiring "experienced only travel agents, or airline personnel." I was neither. However, one agency located near my home (how lucky can you get) had an entry-level position available that involved answering the phone, typing itineraries and packaging tickets. The owner made it very clear this position would never lead to an agent position or agent training, but offered me an interview if I was interested. I was definitely interested! I interviewed and was hired. Bravo, at least I had my foot in the door.

After working on the packaging desk for nine months, I approached the agency owner, and again expressed my desire to become a travel agent. Fortunately, she made an exception and broke her "no experience no training" rules by enrolling me in a United Airlines computer training course. Thus, I realized my dream and became a full-fledged agent.

My confidence and self-worth increased with each error-free reservation and each satisfied customer. I was having a ball! I learned as much as possible about the foreign destinations I booked and got to know my clients well, so their special needs could always be met. I loved my work and took pride in it. I am proud to say, never once did I take the marvelous travel benefits I was receiving for granted. I did keep track of them, however, and received a great deal of satisfaction the year the value of my benefits exceeded my yearly salary. Now that is what I call a job! Way back when I began this career, I could not imagine myself working full time, but just as quickly couldn't visualize myself not working full time, for I was having the time of my life!

What a positive impact those middle-age "hot flashes" had on my life. Ultimately, I became a top-producing corporate international sales agent before my early retirement seventeen years later. I also experienced a world of travel, some shared with family and friends. Most importantly, I proved to myself I could do what I made up my mind to do, no matter how difficult or foreign the task. Yes indeed, life is beautiful and life can begin at forty-plus years of age.

~Carolee Ware
Chicken Soup for the Working Woman's Soul

Over the Wall

I would not have been there except they had lowered the height requirement in the late 1970s to recruit more minorities and women—and I was both a "minority" and a "woman." Their goal was to recruit Asian and Latino men, but it also opened the door for a "little" woman like me to get through. This was my chance—me, Linda Coleman—to become a deputy sheriff.

The day was young and overcast when I arrived at the police academy. But as far as I was concerned, the sun was shining. I'd made it.

It had been a long, grueling year getting to this point. I had taken a written test, a psychological exam and an oral interview, and I had passed all three. Then the background investigation began. They investigated everyone, from my grandmother in Texas, to my next-door neighbors, to the babysitter of my two small children. They knew everything about me from the day I was born.

As part of my qualification process I spent a day at a sheriff station with the captain. I was scrutinized, chastised and downright ostracized. It was no secret how he felt; he never missed an opportunity to tell me. "Women don't belong on the department, all gays should be taken out and shot, where do 'you people' get off thinking you can do whatever you want nowadays?" If I heard one more story about the "good ole days" when women were women and men were men and "you people" knew your place, I think I would have puked.

But all that was behind me now. I was at the academy, and I was going to be a deputy sheriff. My excitement didn't last long.

My first encounter was with a twenty-year career officer, a sergeant nicknamed "Goliath." He was six-feet-four-inches tall, and 300 pounds of solid muscle, to my five-feet-three-inches and 118 pounds of woman. "Sgt. Goliath" let me know in no uncertain terms he was not happy I was there. Like others in the department, he believed this was a "men only" profession. And it would suit many of them just fine if it were "white men only."

The sergeant never called me by name. It was always "little lady" or "little girl." When he looked at me, he would stare as if he were looking right through me. It was apparent he was not going to make it easy. In fact, his job was to make it as difficult as possible for me to pass the physical agility test, and he did a darn good job.

I had to run the mile, climb through one window and out another, walk a balance beam five feet off the ground, pull a 150-pound mannequin thirty yards and push a police car twenty feet, all in record time. And as the sergeant said before I began, "Look here, Little Lady, if you can't do all of these activities including pushing that police car over here until it touches my kneecaps, I'm gonna have the pleasure of sending you home."

I completed each task, but every bone, muscle and fiber of my body ached. I could hardly catch my breath. Some of the recruits passed out and had to be carried off the course. My vision was blurred, my heart beat a mile a minute, and my ears hummed, but I didn't pass out. In fact, I walked off the course on my own and felt pride welling up inside. I had completed that obstacle course, and I was going to be a deputy sheriff.

But the smirk on the sergeant's face told me I was wrong. That's when I discovered yet another challenge waiting for me. This time even I didn't know if I would be able to make it. My head ached, my legs were as heavy as lead, and my arms felt as if someone had yanked them from their sockets.

The ultimate challenge? Climbing a six-foot, solid concrete wall. If somehow you were able to get through the physical agility test, this would separate the boys from the men—or girls from the women, as it were. Recruit after recruit, both men and women, tackled the six-foot wall only to fall to the ground in defeat. Most of them were taller and bigger than me. I could feel my heart sink and my confidence fade. I saw my career with the sheriff's department slipping away.

Two more recruits, and then it would be my turn. I closed my eyes and tried to envision myself going over the wall. Suddenly, I remembered a song my grandmother used to sing in church, an old Negro spiritual. "I shall, I shall, I shall not be moved." My nerves calmed. I heard my father's voice, "You have to be twice as good and do twice as much just to compete." And I thought, I have been twice as good and I have done twice as much and I have given it my all and now this....

And then I swear I heard the words of my high school track coach. "A lady's strength is in her legs, not in her arms." I had watched the women try to tackle the wall by jumping up like the men and grabbing hold of the wall with their arms in an attempt to pull themselves atop the wall, straddle it and drop to the other side. It hadn't worked for them, and I knew it wouldn't work for me.

I shall not be moved. Be twice as good and do twice as much. A lady's strength is in her legs. It was my turn. The six-foot, solid concrete wall loomed bigger than life—the only thing standing between me and my dream. I closed my eyes and imagined it was a track field.

I took off running as fast as I could, and when my feet hit the concrete I looked up to the heavens. And I ran up that wall! I shall not be moved. Twice as good. A lady's strength. I straddled the top and dropped to the other side.

The whole camp was cheering—everyone, that is, except the sergeant. He never said a word. He turned his back and walked away. Several men made it over that day, but I was the only woman.

Since then, I have gone over a lot of walls, but I learned some valuable lessons at the academy that have helped me. What the

Goliaths think is not nearly as important as what I think about myself. The Goliaths despise change and progress, but there are some things even they can't control.

~Linda Coleman-Willis
Chicken Soup for the African American Soul

Woman to Woman

Taking Time for Yourself

I love people. I love my family, my children...
but inside myself is a place where I live all alone
and that's where you renew your springs that never dry up.
~Pearl S. Buck

Calm Mother

*A*s a teenager growing up in the sixties, I knew what I wanted to do with my life and what I didn't want to do. I wanted to travel and see the world. I didn't want to be a mother.

Both desires were a rebellion against my own childhood. I grew up on the flat prairie land of the Midwest and thus yearned to see mountains, clouds and trees. My own parents never treated me well, so I grew up not liking anybody, except for my kind, loving grandmothers.

Every hot, cloudless prairie summer, my family would travel to the tree-lined city to visit both of my grandmothers. Around their own mothers, my parents treated me well. How I loved my grand-mothers! Best of all, they loved me back.

Achieving my teenage goals would be easy: After getting a col-lege degree, I planned to travel to the city of my choice and get a job. After two or three years when I began to get bored, I would move on to another ideal city. If I found my true love along the way, I would get married and settle down, but I wouldn't have children.

In my twenties, I graduated from college and went to live in my chosen city. So far, so good. Then one summer I decided to visit the hot, flat prairie town where I grew up. It was fun to chatter away with the adults I had known as a child. For once, I was being treated like an adult among other adults.

One of the couples I visited asked me if I would babysit for their five little boys. I had never babysat for anyone before. How hard can it be? I thought to myself and accepted.

I found out it could be very hard. I didn't know that five boys, aged two to twelve, could be so loud and energetic. They also got very physical, and amazed as I was, I did not try to control them. This made the situation even worse. Just as the parents walked in through the front door, the little two-year-old boy, who was very wound up, hurled himself onto me trying to greet his parents. Without thinking, I turned around and hit him. The whole family froze in shock. I looked bewildered at everybody until the father asked quietly, "Why did you hit my son?"

"He hit me first," I answered, feeling completely justified.

"It was an accident," he replied.

"It was?"

Violence in my own childhood had been intentional and frequent, never accidental. This new concept had never even occurred to me. I turned toward the little boy and asked, "Did you mean to hit me?"

Still whimpering, he shook his head earnestly, the tears falling down his flushed cheeks. My hardened heart cracked.

"I'm sorry."

The tension relieved, they quickly forgave me and we embraced. Their warmth and forgiveness affected me deeply. I saw that simply not having children wouldn't solve the deeper problems inside me. The abuse I'd experienced as a child had turned me into a violent adult. I couldn't ignore it anymore, but I honestly didn't know what to do. I didn't want to tell anyone, for fear of ruining what few friendships I had. After all, I had almost lost one friendship with a loving family—with one unthinking blow.

The following spring I visited my older brother, who had recently married. He and his wife and child lived on an Indian reservation. I attended church with my family, and found it interesting to be in the minority, one of the few whites among so many Native Americans. During my visit, I befriended an Indian grandmother.

One day, right after church ended, the grandmother and I were standing together and she remarked, "White man's babies are so noisy." Looking around the room at all the contented Indian babies and then at the crying, whimpering white babies, I realized the truth in her words! My nephew was no exception.

"Why is that?" I asked her in astonishment.

She answered by describing the tradition of her tribe. When a young girl started menstruating, she left the tribe for one day to spend time alone in the wilderness and meditate about what kind of woman she would be when she grew up. Of course, her father followed discreetly to ensure her safety.

Each following month, at the appropriate time, she would spend another day by herself and meditate. As she grew, she meditated about what kind of young man she wanted to attract. After engagement, she meditated about what kind of wife she would be. After her marriage, she meditated about what kind of mother she would be, and so on. Thus, each woman took time each month to be alone and meditate about where her life was going, what kind of person she was becoming and what to do about her problems. The grandmother ended her narrative by saying, "Calm mother makes calm baby."

Listening to her, I felt a surge of warmth and love inside me. I knew I had finally discovered the answer to my curse of violence. I followed her advice exactly, only I meditated once a week to make up for the lost years.

First, I meditated on how to be a better worker at my job and how to be a better friend. In the stillness, answers came. I needed to stop taking offense so easily in both situations. I needed to stop thinking and saying "I" so much and start asking about the other person more.

As I was dating, I meditated about each boyfriend and our relationship. Did I give more than I took? Did we laugh easily? Was I a good listener? Did I like him when I wasn't in love with him?

Eventually, I found my true love. After our marriage, I continued the frequent meditations. The process of two becoming one seemed to bring out issues I thought I had resolved sufficiently when I was single. The questions kept coming. However, I stayed calm and stuck with the plan, meditating week by week, month by month.

It's worked! Our marriage has continued happily, and now we have five wonderful children. All of these "white man's babies" have mostly been calm, and the violence of my childhood has remained a thing of the past.

How grateful I am that an old Indian grandmother whose name I never knew managed to change my life and the lives of my children for the better with her simple wisdom: Calm mother makes calm baby.

~Holly Danneman
Chicken Soup for the Mother's Soul 2

It Happened One Autumn

I've been seduced again by the boy next door.

It doesn't happen often, but he does have a way about him. I'm sitting in my office, nose to the grindstone, shoulder pressed to the wheel, struggling to meet deadlines without much success. My brain seems to have slipped into neutral, gone on vacation—oh, you get the idea. So I'm busily shuffling stacks of paper and writing fevered motivational notes to myself: Finish proposal!!!—as if the number of exclamation points will resurrect my will to work.

In the midst of this busy inactivity, I hear a knock on my door. I open it, turn my gaze downward and see Tyler, my young neighbor, and he's holding a football. Somewhat redundantly, he says, "You want to come out and play football with me?"

Tyler is eight, but he knows a playmate when he meets one. The day I moved in, Ty and his brother Jay came over and helped me unload boxes from my U-Haul. After we finished, I bought them each a burger and a root beer. After that, during those first few weeks in my new place, when I needed duct tape or another curtain rod, Ty and Jay were more than willing to accompany me to Wal-Mart and show me the best toys.

Jay is eleven and a cool guy—too cool, actually, to meander over to the lady next door to see if she'll come toss a football with him. Tyler, however, has no such inhibitions. He sees that I have not one, but two bicycles; that I go for walks every day; and that some evenings I sit on my porch and strum on my guitar. So I am, in his eyes, okay.

"Ty," I say, doing my best to be a grown-up, "I really would like to, but I've got to work."

Tyler holds up a piece of white plastic. "Look," he says, as if this piece of conversation will make all the difference: "I got a new tee. I can kick and you can catch."

"Tyler," I repeat slowly, to impress upon him the urgency of my situation. "I have a deadline. That means I have to get this in the mail tomorrow."

"Fifteen minutes," he says steadily, locking my gaze with those cornflower blue eyes.

My children always knew they could do this, too. What kind of signals do I give out, I wonder, that apparently say, "Press on, she can be had?"

I stand in the door, looking at him, considering. Okay, I tell myself, I can go play with Tyler for fifteen minutes and eat dinner at my desk—it's not as if I'm making any progress anyway.

"All right," I respond, wagging a finger. "Let me get my shoes on. But just fifteen minutes. I mean it." Tyler never sees the wagging finger; he's already doing a little end-zone victory dance on my porch.

As I slip on my shoes, my dog enters stage left, positively effervescent. When Bob-Dog sees lace-up shoes come out, he knows the leash is next and then, let the good times roll. So out we go into the front yard—Bob-Dog, Tyler and me. The crystalline air is fresh, cool, filled with the scents of autumn. Leaves crinkle under our feet as Ty kicks off and I dash within the general vicinity of the ball.

"You have to catch it," he says, as if I needed this solemn bit of coaching.

"Thank you, Tyler," I say, as I take up my position down field again.

This time, I catch it and it's my turn to throw. As usual, I toss the football about three feet in front of me. Tyler lopes up beside me in that easy manner of the natural athlete. "The way to do it," he says, picking up the football and demonstrating, "is to twist at the waist before I throw. That way I use more than just my arm."

I try it and I am astounded—I throw the ball halfway across my yard. Not great, but... not utterly pathetic. I try again. Tyler is all over the encouragement thing.

"Way to go!" he says, with absolute sincerity. "Here—throw it all the way down here!"

And so it goes, for about an hour. Finally, my conscience catches up with me. Breathing hard, I tell him it's time to stop.

"Okay," he says, "After you catch one more." He's on very solid turf with that one. He knows I only catch about one out of ten. He tosses. I miss and shag the ball. He tosses, I miss and shag the ball. He tosses and finally I say, "Look, kiddo, I really have to go to work."

He kicks a few leaves and says, "Heck," but then he runs toward the driveway. "Throw long!" he shouts over his shoulder. I do. He misses and I laugh.

Entering the warmth of my house, I remove my jacket—it smells like autumn. My face is cool and I am happy.

Within minutes of sitting down, in a slap-my-forehead, V-8 moment, I suddenly see what my project was missing. Why hadn't I realized that before? Maybe because my body was telling me what my brain didn't want to hear—that recess is important, no matter how old we are or how serious our work becomes.

It's autumn. Front-yard football is best at this time of year and must be savored when in season, just like tomatoes in August or hot cider in December.

I hope I always have a Tyler in my life to remind me that all work and no play make Jill a grumpy girl. I hope that no matter how old I get or how serious I become, that I'll allow myself to be coached—even if the coach is only eight and I can't tell if it's freckles or chocolate milk splattered on his nose.

~K. C. Compton
Chicken Soup to Inspire the Body and Soul

The Wonders of Tupperware

Someone to tell it to is one of the fundamental needs of human beings.
~Miles Franklin

Many years ago, in the far distant past of 1966, Tupperware parties were all the rage with stay-at-home moms. Practically all of us "kept house" then, and these parties gave us a pleasant and acceptable way to go out for the evening, usually leaving the dads to handle the kids' bath and bed routine.

We loved actually talking with people older than five, although our conversations mostly centered around those very topics we knew best — kids and housekeeping. While learning the proper way to "burp" a container, we also discussed burping babies. Usually, after about three hours of listening to the demonstrator, playing silly games and filling out our order forms, we would all go home thinking of the wonderful new plastic additions to our already bulging kitchen storage cabinets. We might not see each other again for a month or so until someone else decided to host the next "party."

One day, after a Thursday night Tupperware party at the home of my friend Kay who lived two doors down from me, I was in the backyard hanging out wash (something else we used to do in the olden days, but that's another story). Kay yelled over the back fence that she had some pastries left over and maybe we should gather up some neighbors and finish them off with coffee later that afternoon. This was an unusual idea in our neighborhood. None of us had lived there very long, we all had little ones who took up a lot of our time and we just didn't socialize much except for demonstration parties. I told Kay it sounded good to me, so we called everyone who had been there the night before and made plans to meet at my house at 2:00.

Normally, by 2:00 in the afternoon, most of us had the kids in for a nap, but this time we decided to forgo the naps for just this once and let them play while we ate the pastries and talked. It was raining out, so the little ones had to play in the dining room of my tiny house, out of sight but within hearing distance, while we moms sat talking in the living room. Before we knew it, two hours had gone by and everyone hurried off to start dinner before the men got home from work. But something interesting had happened in those two hours, something that we all knew we wanted to continue.

We continued to meet for three more years, every Friday afternoon at 2:00, bringing the kids along to scatter toys and grind pretzels into the dining room rug of whoever was hosting that week. We didn't mind the mess—we were learning that sometimes all mothers lose their cool with their kids, sometimes every loving husband was an unfeeling oaf. We weren't alone in the world, and we weren't monsters who sometimes lost control in our frustration with trying to be the best wife and mother. Amazingly, we discovered other women were having the same struggles. And quite often, just talking about it with friends who really knew allowed us to handle things better the next time we felt like throwing in the towel or strangling somebody.

Week by week, my sanity was saved and my marriage was strengthened because I found a safe place to vent my frustrations and learn new ways of coping. We moms learned from each other while we developed wonderful friendships among ourselves, and our children learned valuable social skills (such as picking up your own pretzel crumbs) from their tag-along playgroup. And all because of a Tupperware party!

That Tupperware—who knew it could preserve so many things?

Carol Bryant
Chicken Soup for the Mother's Soul 2

48

Have Freedom, Will Travel

Travel has been my comrade, adventure my inspiration,
accomplishment my recompense.
~Charlotte Cameron

had a ticket. I had my passport. And he had cold feet. I might have known fairy tales don't come true.

Seven months out of my marriage, I had met the "great love of my life." We dated a year. I'd always longed to see Europe, and, with my divorce final, we planned the trip together. Then two weeks before takeoff, he took off. Having piggybacked two breakups, I felt as if I'd been through a double divorce. Here I was, thirty-nine years old, with two small children, and facing my ultimate fear: a life alone.

Was I ready to spend a month in Europe by myself? I had a hard time going to a movie alone! But it did seem now or never. The kids would be with their dad, the money came as part of my property settlement, and I had a job waiting when I returned. Okay, if I was going to be lonely for the next few years, I might as well start by being lonely in Europe.

The highlight of my journey was to be Paris, the city I'd always wanted to see. But now I was frightened to travel without a companion. I steeled myself and went anyway.

I arrived at the train station in Paris panicked and disoriented. I hadn't used my college French in twenty years. Pulling my red suitcase on wobbly wheels behind me, I was shoved and pushed by perspiring travelers reeking of cigarette smoke, different diets and not nearly enough deodorant. The roar of many languages bombarding me seemed unintelligible — just babble.

On my first Metro ride, I encountered an incompetent, clumsy pickpocket. I melted him with a look, and he eased his hand from my purse to fade into the crowded car. At my stop, I hauled my heavy suitcase up the steep stairs and froze.

Cars zoomed helter-skelter, honking belligerently. Somewhere in this confusing city my hotel was hidden, but the directions I had scrawled suddenly weren't legible.

I stopped two people. Both greeted me with that Parisian countenance that said: "Yes, I speak English, but you'll have to struggle with your French if you want to talk to me." I walked up one street and across another. A wheel broke off my suitcase. When I finally found the hotel, my heart was pounding, I was sweating like a basketball player and my spirits drooped. They flattened altogether when I saw my room.

I couldn't stay. Could I? The wallpaper looked like it had been through a fire. The bedsprings creaked. The bathroom was down the hall, and the window looked out onto the brick wall of another building. Welcome to Paris.

I sincerely wanted to die. I missed my friend. I was entering my third week away from home and my kids, and I had arrived in the most romantic city in the world, alone. Alone and lonely. Alone, lonely and petrified.

The most important thing I did in Paris happened at that moment. I knew that if I didn't go out, right then, and find a place to have dinner, I would hide in this cubicle my entire time in Paris. My dream would be foregone, and I might never learn to enjoy the world as a single individual. So I pulled myself together and went out.

Evening in Paris was light and balmy. When I reached the Tuileries, I strolled along a winding path, listening to birds sing, watching children float toy sailboats in a huge fountain. No one seemed to be in a hurry. Paris was beautiful. And I was here alone but suddenly not lonely. My sense of accomplishment at overcoming my fear and vulnerability had left me feeling free, not abandoned.

I wore out two pairs of shoes during my week's stay in Paris. I did everything there was to do, and it was the greatest week of my European vacation. I returned home a believer in the healing power of solitary travel. Years later, I still urge divorcing or widowed friends to take their solo flight in the form of travel plans.

Those who have gone have returned changed—even by a four-day weekend in Santa Fe, an Amtrak ride up the coast or an organized tour of Civil War battlefields. Traveling alone redeems itself by demanding self-reliance and building the kind of confidence that serves the single life well.

Certainly Paris became my metaphor for addressing life's challenges on my own. Now when I meet an obstacle I just say to myself: If I can go to Paris, I can go anywhere.

~Dawn McKenna
Chicken Soup for the Single's Soul

49

Message in a Body

Take care of your body. It's the only place you have to live.
~Jim Rohn

*H*ave you completely lost your mind? I asked myself as I walked down the hall to the office of my boss. In my right hand I clutched the resignation letter I had typed the night before.

No, you haven't, the small part of me that wasn't scared to death whispered back. Remember what happened a few months ago?

Oh yes, I remembered it well.

I had worked for the same company for over a decade, my dedication and long hours finally paying off when I was promoted to upper management while still young. I had tons of responsibilities, and there were deadlines and daily crises. The stacks of paper on my desk grew taller as the weeks passed, and phone calls, faxes and e-mails dominated my life. I took great pride in my work, and mailed home some business cards to my parents so they could see the title under my name.

One by one, relationships with friends dwindled as I lived and breathed my job. It had become my whole life, and I gave it 110 percent. I pumped myself up with caffeine during the day and took over-the-counter sleep aids to fall asleep at night. I had five kinds of headache remedies and dozens of antacids in my purse as I pushed myself beyond my limits. I started keeping a pad and pen near my bed so I could take notes during those middle-of-the-night anxiety attacks that started to plague me.

Finally, my body said, No more! I had taken three days off and planned to go to Florida and soak in the tranquility of sun, ocean and beach, but the morning I was scheduled to leave I couldn't even get up. My body refused to move. I was utterly exhausted and drained. I slept all day, getting up only to eat before collapsing back into bed. The next day the same thing happened. I tried to bribe my body by imagining a dazzling mental slide show of our vacation, but my body said, Thanks, but no thanks. I need to be where I am.

By the third day I was scared. After forty-eight hours of almost nonstop sleep I was still exhausted and unwilling to move, so I called my doctor, and his office worked me into their schedule.

I lay on the examining table while a technician ran blood tests. I caught a glimpse of myself in a mirror and was shocked—an older woman stared back at me. Who are you? I wondered. She didn't answer. The doctor came back in and pronounced me the healthiest sick person he had ever seen. "You have hyperstress," he said, and wrote a prescription.

"What am I supposed to take?" I asked. In a barely legible scrawl he had written on the pad: "Get a different job."

That day I made a promise to myself: I will carve out time for myself every day. When the clock says it's 5 P.M., I will leave, no matter what.

The first day back at work I had to force myself to do it, and was actually shocked when the sky didn't fall. What a revelation!

I started walking my dogs again, trying to pay them back for all the times I'd left them. I picked up my journal, blew dust off the cover and began writing. Words came slowly at first, then more freely as my inner voice was finally allowed to speak. During the next three months it said: quit your job, over and over again.

I'd been working since I was seventeen, part-time to put myself though college, and then full-time immediately after graduation. Now I had a strong feeling there was a person under all those diplomas and titles who was literally dying to get out. So, with no firm plans for the future, I gave a thirty-day notice and then spent that month alternating between panic, regret and hysteria. The real shocker—that I was easily replaceable—came when the company filled my position two weeks after my notice. The last day on the job I looked into the bathroom mirror and asked: Who are you?

The silence was deafening.

Suddenly, I had no job on which to hang my identity; I was putting all my trust in the great unknown, and I was truly scared. But there was also a strange, previously unknown faith buoying me up, telling me, Don't be afraid. Everything will work out. Believe in yourself! I clung to that like a frightened child to her mother's hand.

Finally, I was free to embark on my journey of self-discovery. After a while, I realized I'd never really forgotten who I was—I had just covered it up with work, work and more work. As I took long, slow walks in the woods, I rediscovered my inner core. I listened to my body and slept when it was tired, ate when it was hungry. I reconnected with friends, read dozens of books and wrote in my journal.

That faith did not fail me. Two months later, a friend heard of a low-stress job and helped me get an interview. I got the job—and a hefty pay cut as well—but I don't regret it for a second. That eight-week sabbatical changed my life and taught me that a life without balance isn't worth living—it isn't even livable! I felt a profound gratefulness to my body for sending me such a clear message.

I had dipped my hand in the well of restoration, and I will never forget it. I had finally learned to define myself from the inside out, rather than the outside in.

~Kelly L. Stone
Chicken Soup to Inspire the Body and Soul

Chapter 10

Woman to Woman

Gratitude

*Help your brother's boat across and
your own will reach the shore.*
~Hindu Proverb

First Pick

"We'll each pick a number, starting from oldest to youngest, then we'll each take a pick, in the order of our numbers. You understand?" Louise was fully in charge. We were taking our pick of Mama's quilts.

None of us wanted to fight. Five sisters and one brother were trying valiantly to honor and respect our parents. Louise is the oldest and had the most daily contact with our mother before her quick death from cancer, long quietly taking over her body, but not loud enough to be noticed until too late. Here we sat, on a cold October day, six middle-aged children in the living room of our youth, with eyes red with grief and nervous sweaty hands.

These last six quilts our mother made were something we needed to be fair about and they were all laid out for our choosing. Although not works of art for the most part, they were our heritage. There was a queen-size Dresden plate and two twin-size patchworks, both in good shape. A double-size, double-knit polyester little girl quilt that we remembered from the era of leisure suits and a queen-size log cabin that told its age by the colors: orange and avocado. Then there was the quilt on my mother's bed, a double-size star pattern of Wedgwood blue chintz and cotton. It was gorgeous. And it smelled like Mama.

We reached into the shoebox one at a time for our numbers, and being the baby, I picked last. Fitting, as I got number six, the last to choose from the bed-cover legacy. Libby was the first, and no one was surprised to watch her gather up the Wedgwood blue chintz and fold it into her bag. When my turn came, the double-knit polyester quilt was left, so I took it, remembering Mother handstitching the pitiful thing. So much work for so little beauty! We'll keep it in the car, I thought to myself, for a picnic blanket.

As the holidays approached, our grief stayed with us, mostly hidden, but popping up unannounced as tears over a remembered song or a phone call impossible to make. We all moved our bodies toward Christmas, even as our minds stayed with Mother in her hospital bed before she died, or in her flower garden—or on her sun porch. Christmas would be hard.

Packages began to arrive, though, and I had to notice that the rest of the world didn't stop in the shadow of my sadness. On Christmas Eve, my children have the privilege of opening one package before bed, but on this night they encouraged me to join in. A large box from Ohio had piqued their interest. What could Aunt Libby have sent?

Laughing, I tore open the box, expecting a joke: an inflatable chair or bubble bath buried in yards of newspaper. As I peeked past the wrapping, my hands shook and my vision wavered through a film of sudden tears. Inside the box lay, neatly folded, the coveted chintz quilt from Mama's bed. I buried my face in the folds to take in the lingering scent of my mother, and to add my tears. On top of the quilt was a card:

To my baby sister—my first pick.

~René J. Manley
Chicken Soup for the Soul Celebrates Sisters

51

The Scar

Everything has beauty, but not everyone sees it.
~Confucius

His thumb softly rubbed the twisted flesh on my cheek. The plastic surgeon, a good fifteen years my senior, was a very attractive man. His masculinity and the intensity of his gaze seemed almost overpowering.

"Hmmm," he said quietly. "Are you a model?"

Is this a joke? Is he kidding? I asked myself, and I searched his handsome face for signs of mockery. No way would anyone ever confuse me with a fashion model. I was ugly. My mother casually referred to my sister as her pretty child. Anyone could see I was homely. After all, I had the scar to prove it.

The accident happened in fourth grade, when a neighbor boy picked up a hunk of concrete and heaved the mass through the side of my face. An emergency room doctor stitched together the shreds of skin, pulling cat-gut through the tattered outside of my face and then suturing the shards of flesh inside my mouth. For the rest of the year, a huge bandage from cheekbone to jaw covered the raised angry welt.

A few weeks after the accident, an eye exam revealed I was nearsighted. Above the ungainly bandage sat a big, thick pair of glasses. Around my head, a short fuzzy glob of curls stood out like mold growing on old bread. To save money, Mom had taken me to a beauty school where a student cut my hair. The overzealous girl hacked away cheerfully. Globs of hair piled up on the floor. By the time her instructor wandered over, the damage was done. A quick conference followed, and we were given a coupon for a free styling on our next visit.

"Well," sighed my father that evening, "you'll always be pretty to me," and he hesitated, "even if you aren't to the rest of the world."

Right. Thanks. As if I couldn't hear the taunts of the other kids at school. As if I couldn't see how different I looked from the little girls whom the teachers fawned over. As if I didn't occasionally catch a glimpse of myself in the bathroom mirror. In a culture that values beauty, an ugly girl is an outcast. My looks caused me no end of pain. I sat in my room and sobbed every time my family watched a beauty pageant or a "talent" search show.

Eventually I decided that if I couldn't be pretty, I would at least be well-groomed. Over the course of years, I learned to style my hair, wear contact lenses and apply make-up. Watching what worked for other women, I learned to dress myself to best advantage. And now, I was engaged to be married. The scar, shrunken and faded with age, stood between me and a new life.

"Of course, I'm not a model," I replied with a small amount of indignation.

The plastic surgeon crossed his arms over his chest and looked at me appraisingly. "Then why are you concerned about this scar? If there is no professional reason to have it removed, what brought you here today?"

Suddenly he represented all the men I'd ever known. The eight boys who turned me down when I invited them to the girls-ask-boys dance. The sporadic dates I'd had in college. The parade of men who had ignored me since then. The man whose ring I wore on my left hand. My hand rose to my face. The scar confirmed it; I was ugly. The room swam before me as my eyes filled with tears.

The doctor pulled a rolling stool up next to me and sat down. His knees almost touched mine. His voice was low and soft.

"Let me tell you what I see. I see a beautiful woman. Not a perfect woman, but a beautiful woman. Lauren Hutton has a gap between her front teeth. Elizabeth Taylor has a tiny, tiny scar on her forehead," he almost whispered. Then he paused and handed me a mirror. "I think to myself how every remarkable woman has an imperfection, and I believe that imperfection makes her beauty more remarkable because it assures us she is human."

He pushed back the stool and stood up. "I won't touch it. Don't let anyone fool with your face. You are delightful just the way you are. Beauty really does come from within a woman. Believe me. It is my business to know."

Then he left.

I turned to the face in the mirror. He was right. Somehow over the years, that ugly child had become a beautiful woman. Since that day in his office, as a woman who makes her living speaking before hundreds of people, I have been told many times by people of both sexes that I am beautiful. And, I know I am.

When I changed how I saw myself, others were forced to change how they saw me. The doctor didn't remove the scar on my face; he removed the scar on my heart.

~Joanna Slan
A Second Chicken Soup for the Woman's Soul

52

A Boy's Bike

I grew up in the small town of Cazenovia located smack in the middle of New York State. At thirteen, I met Ruth, a girl with a personality like an unbroken mare, wild and unpredictable. We became fast friends.

Ruth had a way of convincing me to do things I normally would not do. For example, when my parents were going to buy me a new bicycle, I had planned to get a regular girl's bike, the one without the top crossbar. Ruth suggested a boy's bike instead. I was scared of that horribly high top bar. I just knew I'd fall flat on my face trying to get my leg over it. Ruth convinced me I could do it, and soon a blue ten-speed boy's bike became my pride and joy.

Ruth and I rode our ten-speeds everywhere—around town, around the lake, into the hills, and over to Syracuse and back. We even bought saddlebags and racks so we could carry gear for overnight trips. For us, there was no greater pleasure than climbing on our bikes and heading off for a twenty-mile jaunt.

One day I heard a story about a group who had ridden from Buffalo to Albany, along the old Erie Canal tow path. The idea of a long-distance bicycle trip captured my imagination. So it was I who talked Ruth into doing something—a five-day tour to Buffalo and back, halfway across the state. We could stay with my grandparents in Rochester and Buffalo.

Plans were made. We got maps, put together gear and set the

date. We were all ready for our trip when, suddenly, Ruth's parents told her she couldn't go. So ended our bike tour before it began.

Grudgingly, I accepted that we were not going on our long-distance bike tour, but in the back of my mind I knew that someday I would.

Years later I got married, moved to San Diego, and had a successful career, a nice car and a wonderful house—everything the yuppie could ever desire. I convinced Brian, my husband, to buy a ten-speed bike, and most Saturday mornings we would go riding somewhere out in the country.

It wasn't too long before memories of that aborted bike trip returned, and my yearning to do it grew. But this time, my ambitions were much higher, a coast-to-coast ride. So one day I said to Brian, "Somehow all this riding doesn't seem worthwhile unless we're going somewhere. What would you think about riding cross-country?"

I couldn't believe it when Brian said, without hesitation, "Sure."

Soon we were selecting routes, buying new bikes, borrowing equipment, arranging time off from work, and training, training, training. We were excited, yet at the same time, we were somewhat apprehensive.

How would we do? Could we handle sitting on the seat of a bicycle day after day, mile after mile? Would we get injured or sick? Could we tolerate whatever Mother Nature could throw at us? What about those infamous headwinds of the plains? Would they force us to quit? Is two months long enough? And would we still be talking to each other at the end?

On August 5, 1988, after months of preparation, we turned our first pedal and our journey of four thousand miles began with just one push.

Two months later, on October 2, we arrived in Bar Harbor, Maine—safe, pooped and still very much in love. In fact, on that first day out of Bellingham, while riding on a quiet road along the Skagit River, Brian had made a prediction: "This could be addictive." And it was.

By the time we reached Bar Harbor, we were hooked. As we

pushed our bikes down to the water's edge to dip the wheels in the Atlantic Ocean, I kept repeating, "I wish we could take a week rest and then keep on going." Jobs, a new house, car payments and one cat awaited us in San Diego. We had to go back. But a new dream had begun to form for both of us—a worldwide bike journey.

For the next eight years, we continued taking short bicycle trips, a few weeks each year. Yet our dream of a worldwide bike tour persisted. We knew that riding around the world at a pace that would allow us to explore would take many years.

Could we gather the money to allow us this amount of time? How much would it take? While bicycling can be cheap—basic food and camping is about all that's required—it does take some capital. So we started saving.

We sold our house, all our furniture and our cars—almost everything we owned. It was heart-wrenching. We gave away or sold everything that had defined our lives for nearly fifteen years. But we had our goal: We knew what we wanted to do and that kept us going.

I often felt frustrated, angry and depressed, questioning if we would ever be able to do it. I had heard that if you have a goal, you need to place some item that represents that goal, in a place where you see it each and every day. Otherwise it can easily get lost in the shuffle of day-to-day life. So, in my office, right in front of me, I hung a poster of a bike tourist riding up the Going-to-the-Sun Highway in Glacier National Park. This poster was my reminder. I'd look at it, say to myself, Soon. It's not far off, regain my composure and get back to the job at hand.

On August 3, 1995, in sweltering heat just outside Denver, Colorado, we climbed aboard our loaded bicycles and took off on a journey around the world.

Two years later, on October 9, 1997, after riding through Mexico, Belize and Guatemala, and up the East Coast, we rode into the small town of Cazenovia, New York.

There, after so many years, I pulled up at Ruth's house, on my "boy's bike."

As I walked up to the door, I recounted all the miles I had clocked since that bike trip she and I never took. I could feel tears welling up inside me as I rang the bell and awaited the familiar face of my childhood friend and the opportunity to thank her for pointing me in the right direction.

~Caryl Bergeron
Chicken Soup for the Traveler's Soul

My Family Was Separated

Is solace anywhere more comforting than in the arms of a sister.
~Alice Walker

My family was separated and placed into foster care when I was five years old. We grew up living in separate homes, never knowing each other. As I grew older, the only memory that remained of my family was of a tall, slender woman always being there to comfort me. In my mind, this woman was my mother. I believed that someday she would return and life would be normal again. She was in my prayers throughout my childhood.

On Thanksgiving Day, which was also my forty-fifth birthday, there wasn't much to celebrate. My son was moving to another state, and I was feeling not only older but also sad to be losing the closeness of the only family I knew. A card arrived in the mail with a return name and address of someone I didn't recognize. Opening it, I found a Thanksgiving wish with a short note reading, "I was thinking of you on your birthday, Mom." The memories of the tall, slender woman flashed through my mind. My feelings felt like a roller coaster going from anger to extreme happiness in moments. If this was my mother, why had she abandoned us? Why didn't she ever come to get me? Why would she be writing now, after all these years? At the same time, I wanted to hear her voice and feel her warmth.

For two weeks, the card lay on the table tearing at my heart. Finally, summing up the courage to call information, I got her number.

Holding my breath and trying to calm my heart, I dialed. On the fifth ring, I felt relief that no one was answering. Then, just as I was about to hang up, a voice from the past said, "Hello." Unsure of what to say, I asked to whom I was speaking. It turned out to be my older sister who was cleaning out our mother's apartment. Two weeks after sending the card, Mom had died.

As we talked, reacquainting ourselves, I asked what my mom looked like. My sister was surprised that I didn't remember. She told me Mom was a very short, stocky lady. Then who was the tall, slender woman that I remember?

As we continued our conversation, our family and our life began returning to me.

My older sister was seven when our mother left us. For two years, she was the one caring for us, keeping us safe, cooking our meals and drying our tears. She was the one holding me at night when nightmares woke me, singing me songs, wiping my tears when I was scared. It was my sister who told me to run and lock myself in the bathroom as she tried to keep foster care from taking us away.

We talked for hours that night, reminiscing about the past. She had found our brother and baby sister, and we made plans to reunite after forty years of separation. Neither one of us wanted the night to end, but as dawn approached we finally gave in. "By the way," I asked before hanging up, "how tall are you?"

She answered, "Five-foot-nine, why?"

"Because you were the tall, slender woman who made the difference in my life." She was crying as I said, "Good night, I love you."

~Nora Steuber-Tamblin
Chicken Soup for the Sister's Soul

54

Tearing Down the Wall

Forgiveness does not change the past, but it does enlarge the future.
~Paul Boese

There was a moment, a day, when I first discovered that my father was famous. I was about five years old, and my parents had taken me to Disneyland. We were waiting to get on the Teacup ride when dozens of people realized that Ronald Reagan, the host of General Electric Theater, was there. We were suddenly surrounded by eager, smiling faces and arms begging for my father's autograph.

I remember looking up at my handsome father and feeling frightened that he was being taken from me, claimed by strangers, swallowed by the crowd.

Daughters lean toward their fathers in ways that they never do with mothers: tenderly, with unrequited longing. If that father is famous, the longing for him cuts deeper until it is a river running through your life, drowning every other relationship.

I was fourteen when my father was elected governor of California; I knew there would be no turning back. Politics is a demanding mistress and for eight years, California was my father's other child. I was consumed with sibling rivalry; I was angry, petulant. I wanted more of him, his time, his attention. I lashed out bitterly, tearfully, hurting him with my defiance, all the while loving him desperately. My real fury was at the life of public service I believed had taken him from me.

When he was elected president in 1981, America was now the favored child, or so I believed. During his two terms in office, I felt that when I reached for him, all I could grasp was his shadow.

I got my revenge with other men. I frequently chose ones whose lives had no opening for me, oftentimes, married men. Or I would set my sights on men who had no ambition, no future. Either way, they were stand-ins for the man who once taught me to ride a horse and swim in the ocean, who climbed hills with me on windy days to fly a kite and who could find Pegasus in a sky full of stars. I used other men to act out my rage, but the two who really suffered were my father and me.

The problem was that I hadn't separated the private man from the public figure. I had been looking at my father's chosen profession and goals as a type of larceny; they were stealing him from me. It took me many years to understand that the shadow people cast in the world is a part of them.

All the while I thought my father had abandoned me. The truth was that I had abandoned him.

I returned as he was starting to leave, pulled away not by his duty or his country, but by a disease. I have returned with a reverence for the life he lived: for the persistence of his dreams and the unfailing faith that let him burn past his history as a poor kid from a dusty Midwest town, past those who scoffed about an actor becoming president, past those who said his passion was just pretense. He proved them all wrong, and his absence left a hole in the world now that he is gone.

History will immortalize Ronald Reagan as the president who helped end the Cold War, who stood in front of the Berlin Wall and said, "Mr. Gorbachev, tear down this wall." As his daughter, I immortalize him in the quiet passages of my heart. By instructing me in the rhythms of nature, my father taught me about life. By waiting for me, the prodigal child, to come back, he taught me patience. I live my life differently for having known him. As dramatically as the Berlin Wall came down, the walls between us crumbled and I stood on open ground, wondering why I had ever put up walls at all.

After the anger, after the ranting and acting out, we finally grow up and we realize it's a gift to be born to someone who dreams big and reaches far. It inspires us to do the same, because their blood runs through us, and the lessons they pass on to us are powerful.

~Patti Davis
Chicken Soup for the Father & Daughter Soul

55

Twins Entwined

"Diane! Marsha! You girls get on in here. Supper's on the table!" My sister and I glanced up, quickly and silently signaling each other for a race to the back door. My grandmother stood there, one hand on her hip and the other shielding her eyes from the summer sun. She was heaven in a housedress. She smelled of Jergen's Lotion, chocolate-covered cherries and TubeRose snuff. We worshipped her.

I won the race, almost tackling Nannie in the doorway.

"My Lord, hon, look at you!" she scolded as she pulled me back for inspection. Then her gaze turned to Marsha, who had finally reached the steps. "Now look at your sister. How come she looks like a little lady?"

As we sat down at the dinner table, I shot a look at Marsha. We were twins, joined at the soul from the moment we took our first breaths. We were supposed to be the same, but we weren't—not by a long shot. Marsha loved lace, velvet, patent leather shoes and all of the things girls were supposed to like. She could sit for hours drawing paper dolls, designing their elaborate wardrobes and cutting out all of the patterns with precision.

I was a tomboy. I had a passion for trees and had conquered each and every one in our neighborhood. No boy could climb higher or faster.

I closed my eyes and started to pray that Marsha might be more like me. But then it occurred to me that we were okay with who we each were. I made the mud pies, and she decorated them with pebbles and rose petals. We found ways to work around our differences.

Years passed. We both grew up, married and took on the trappings of responsibility. No more climbed trees or paper dolls.

Somehow during those years, my sweet, prim, spotless sister became a gardener. The child who would never jump into a rain puddle or pat out a mud pie now reveled in the earth. But I, the one who had practically eaten the outdoors every day, shunned it. I was an adult now, after all.

I would shake my head in disbelief when I saw her bury her hands in the soil. When she rattled off the names of her roses, I'd roll my eyes. "I'll never relate to this, Marsha. A rose is a rose!"

So many other things taxed our childhood connection. Finally a time came when it seemed as though our special bond could never be repaired or regained. I had been divorced for years, struggling to raise my son on my own and bouncing from one relationship to the next. My sister was a counselor on a community hotline for battered women. She saw the signs in my life way before I did. She told me — but I didn't want to hear. By the time I realized that she spoke the truth, I had made her the enemy. I ignored the fact that the man that I was living with was methodically and systematically chipping away at my self, at my own identity.

Things got worse. Each day, my only goal was survival. My soul went underground. Finally, one morning while I was getting ready for work, I looked into the mirror and didn't recognize the person staring back at me. Something inside of me snapped. I had to find a way out or die. I called my sister. Although we only lived a few blocks from one another, it had been four years since we had last spoken.

Marsha came to me without hesitation. We agreed that I had to move out, yet I was nearly penniless. I started spending every spare moment looking for a place to live, all the while worrying how I could afford it.

One particular night, after I'd just finished another disappointing search through the real estate ads, my sister called.

"Get dressed, kiddo. I'm coming to get you."

As we drove off in the darkness, I asked Tony, her husband, "What gives? Where are we going?"

All he said was, "Just wait, Diane, you'll see."

We turned down a street and pulled up in front of a house that looked just like the house my grandmother had once owned. It was in disrepair and looked as if it had been vacant for years. The yard was barren—just like my life, I thought. But the place called to me. I knew it was meant to be mine.

Tony worked with someone who knew the owner and persuaded him to rent the property to me, cheap. Marsha's only request was that I let the garden be hers. No problem. I had no interest in it.

On the move-in day, Marsha arrived with a plan showing the beds of the garden, but she said that the choice of plants would be mine.

"I don't know a daffodil from a clump of crab grass," I told her. "You figure it out."

"No," she replied. "This is your playground. The plants have to suit you, not me." I thought she was nuts, but I went along.

We started the garden just days after I moved in. I went to the nursery with her and tried picking by color. I'd point to something and Marsha would shake her head and pass it by, or smile and put it in the cart. It amazed me that you had to buy soil! I was totally ignorant of the process. I thought that things just grew!

Together, we loaded everything in the car and headed for home. We chatted about our purchases and joked about my gardening ignorance. As we pulled into the driveway of my "new" home, I suddenly realized I had not been frightened or unhappy that day—not once.

And then something more happened. There is a moment for each of us that transforms us—a moment just as mundane as any other, but a moment that will forever be etched in your mind just the same. Mine came as I tugged the huge bag of soil over to Marsha. She was on her knees, weeding out a bed we were planting.

"Open it and dump it right here," she demanded.

"The whole thing?" I asked.

"Yep," she said. "The whole darn thing."

I took off my shoes and stood in the midst of the flower bed we were constructing. Then I slit the bag and let the soil cascade down my legs and bury my feet. As the sensation of the warm dirt traveled across my skin, something clicked in my memory: all of those days when I had gone barefoot as a child, and how much I had loved to feel mud squish between my toes. Suddenly I plopped down in the middle of all that dirt and looked directly at my sister.

She knew something had happened. As our eyes held, I reached down and picked up a handful of earth and made a perfect little pie. With tears in her eyes, she looked down beside her, picked up a small pebble and placed it right in the middle of my creation.

We sat there in the warm earth, two grown women streaked with dirt and tears, awed by the love that had never really left us. At that moment, we knew without words that we had come full circle. Nothing on this earth would ever separate us again.

Now as I weed in the fragrant peace of my garden, I realize that there is still a lot of work to be done—in my garden and in my life. But thanks to a sister who wouldn't let go, we're growing just fine, both my garden and I.

~Diane C. Daniels
Chicken Soup for the Gardener's Soul

Chicken Soup for the Soul

If you have enjoyed this book
or it has touched your life in some way,
we would love to hear from you.

Please send your comments to:
Hallmark Book Feedback
P.O. Box 419034
Mail Drop 215
Kansas City, MO 64141

Or e-mail us at:
booknotes@hallmark.com